Journeyman Electrician Test Study Guide!
Crash Course to Help You Prep for the Electrical Exam!

Jeff Voitkovyak

"Electrical work design can be learned but the experience is required to work in a live line."

Table of Contents

Chapter 1 – Introduction   7

    What is a Journeyman Electrician Exam?   7

    How to Sign Up for the Journeyman Electrician Exam   9

    How to Prepare for the Journeyman Electrician Exam   10

    How to Use the Index   12

Chapter 2 – Ohm's Law   15

    What is Ohm's Law?   15

    The History of Ohm's Law   16

    Breaking Down the Ohm's Law Pyramid   17

    Practice Questions: Ohm's Law   18

    Answer Key: Ohm's Law   20

Chapter 3 – Electrical Theory   23

    The Three Primary Forces   23

        Current   23

        Voltage   24

        Impedance   24

    Reactance   25

        Inductive Reactance   25

        Capacitive Reactance   26

        Practice Questions: Reactance   27

        Answer Key: Reactance   28

    Electric Power   30

        Reactive Power   32

        Real Power   32

        Apparent Power   33

Practice Questions: Electric Power	34
Answer Key: Electric Power	35
Electric Charge	**36**
Practice Questions: Electric Charge	39
Answer Key: Electric Charge	40
Power Efficiency	**41**
Practice Questions: Power Efficiency	43
Answer Key: Power Efficiency	44
Power Factor	**45**
Practice Questions: Power Factor	49
Answer Key: Power Factor	50

Chapter 4 – Codes — *52*

Electrical Codes	**52**
International Codes	**53**
The Eleven Components of the NEC	**54**
How to Understand the Terms and Concepts of the Code Book	**60**
How to Tab the Code Book	**61**
How to Highlight Key Information on the Code Book	**63**
Methods of Looking Up Answers in the Code Book	**64**
Practice Questions Set A: Codes	**66**
Practice Questions Set B: Codes	**78**
Answer Key Set A: Codes	**90**
Answer Key Set B: Codes	**96**

Chapter 5 – Electrical Calculations & Load Calculations — *103*

Box Fill Calculations	**105**
Examples of Box Fill Calculations	106

Practice Questions: Box Fill Calculations	110
Answer Key: Box Fill Calculations	111

Conduit Fill Calculations — 114

Examples of Conduit Fill Calculations	117
Practice Questions: Conduit Fill Calculations	120
Answer Key: Conduit Fill Calculations	121

Conductor Calculations — 124

Conductor Ampacity	124
Conductor Size	125
Conductor Protection	126
Practice Questions: Conductor Calculations	126
Answer Key: Conductor Calculations	127

Motor Calculations — 128

Motor Load	128
Motor Conductors	132
Motor Overload Protection	134
Short-Circuit and Ground-Fault Protection	134
Practice Questions: Motor Calculations	135
Answer Key: Motor Calculations	136

Branch Circuit Calculations — 138

Practice Questions: Branch Circuit Calculations	139
Answer Key: Branch Circuit Calculations	140

Dwelling Load Calculations — 140

One-Family Dwelling Units	140
Multifamily Dwelling Units	147
Practice Questions: Dwelling Load Calculations	153
Answer Key: Dwelling Load Calculations	155

Commercial Load Calculations — **158**
- Specific Loads — 159
- Receptacle Loads — 160
- Electric Sign Loads — 160
- Practice Questions: Commercial Load Calculations — 161
- Answer Key: Commercial Load Calculations — 161

Voltage Drop Calculations — **163**
- Formulas for a Single-Phase Circuit — 164
- Formulas for a 3-Phase Circuit — 166
- Formulas for Percentage of Voltage Drop — 167
- Practice Questions: Voltage Drop Calculations — 168
- Answer Key: Voltage Drop Calculations — 169

Chapter 1 – Introduction

You have made the right decision to prepare for the Journeyman Electrician Exam with the help and guidance of this book. Before delving into the topics that will be covered in the exam, you should keep in mind the following points to set your expectations about what this book can do for you:

- Explain the various concepts, theories, and formulas so that you can arrive at the right answer
- Provide sample questions that are similar to the ones that will be asked during the licensing exam
- Demonstrate how the National Electrical Code and its index should be used as a reference for the exam

As you can see, this book aims to boost your chances of passing the Journeyman Electrician Exam to obtain your license. Take note that being licensed and being an excellent electrician are two separate things. You need to put in the effort and complete real-life projects to gain a holistic understanding of this industry.

Moreover, using this self-study guide does not completely guarantee a passing score for the licensing exam. Again, you have to make an effort in absorbing the information presented to you, and apply the tips and tricks that will be shared with you throughout this book.

For the first chapter, you will be given an overview of the Journeyman Electrician Exam and how you can sign up for it. The latter part of the chapter deals with the things you have to do to prepare for the exam itself, including how to use the index of the NEC.

The final section of this chapter contains tips, hints, and reminders that will prove to be practical and valuable while you are taking the exam. By the end of this introduction, you are going to have a more solid idea about what to expect from the Journeyman Electrician Exam as well as the preparatory work that you must go through to secure your license.

What is a Journeyman Electrician Exam?

To ensure safety and uphold professionalism, the state or local government requires all apprentices who intend to work as licensed electricians to undergo the Journeyman Electrician Examination. The contents of this exam are based on the general electrical theory and the NEC—which is a set of standards, rules, and regulations that apply to electrical designs and installations of wiring and equipment in the USA. Through this exam, the state will be able to assess if the individual has a sufficient understanding of the code and the technical aspects of operating and installing electrical wires and equipment.

The Journeyman Electrician Exam consists of a series of tests about the different sections of the NEC, as well as basic electrical engineering concepts. Each state has its version of the exam, however, so it is best to contact the licensing department or the testing company of your state to be sure.

The variations are only minimal in most cases though. Expect around 80 to 100 test items—most of which are multiple-choice questions. Depending on the length of the exam, it may take you about 240 minutes to finish it.

Typical subject areas that are covered in a Journeyman Electrician Exam are as follow:

- Electrical Definitions
- Electrical Engineering Theories
- Different Types of Electrical Calculations
- Electrical Plans
- Electrical Feeders and Services
- Electrical Equipment and Devices
- Electrical Wiring Methods and Materials
- Branch Circuit and Conductors
- Motors, Controllers, and Generators
- Special Occupancies and Equipment

> **Take Note!**
>
> A licensed journeyman electrician must still conduct their electrical works under the guidance of a master electrician. The requirements to level up your license to a master electrician depend on the state where you operate.
>
> In general, however, you need to have a degree in electrical engineering. You should also maintain your journeyman electrician license for no less than two years before your application.
>
> Since the license is valid for only one year, this means you would have to take the Journeyman Electrician Exam twice to be considered eligible for the Master Electrician Exam. In terms of practical experience, a minimum of 12,000 hours of work that had been supervised by a master electrician is required.

The results of the exam are given right away because it is administered using a computer. A printout of the official test score report must be submitted to the testing site, however. The passing score for the Journeyman Electrician Exam is 70%.

Upon passing the exam, a license shall be issued by the state to serve as a guarantee to their customers that the person bearing the license can complete projects that are safe, practical, and economical.

How to Sign Up for the Journeyman Electrician Exam

First of all, you cannot just walk into an examiner's office and ask to be included in their testing schedule. Instead, you need to secure permission from the examination board beforehand. This involves filling up the application form for the exam and paying the non-refundable application fee of around $75 per individual.

The instructions for the application form may vary from state to state, but in general, you will be required to provide the following information:

- Your Full Legal Name
- Date of Birth
- Gender
- Social Security Number
- Mailing Address
- Physical Address of Your Residence
- Home or Office Phone Number
- Personal or Work Email Address
- Criminal History
- Disciplinary Action History
- Employment History

One of the purposes of the application is to verify if you had completed at least 8,000 hours of practical training under a master electrician who had received their license from the same state that will administer your Journeyman Electrician Exam. An early-exam option may be requested if you had at least 7,000 hours of on-the-job training experience, too.

Therefore, the application form must be supported by an Experience Verification Form that is signed by your supervising master electrician. In case you cannot contact your supervisor, you may request the assistance of the electrical contractor that the master electrician had worked with to reach out to them. If that still did not work for you, then you may try searching for the master electrician's contact information in the License Search database of the Licensing and Regulation Department of your state.

Once you have submitted the requirements, your application will be reviewed by the examination board. If your application has been approved, you will receive a notification via physical mail or email. As such, the contact information you provide in your application form must be complete and accurate.

Scheduling of the Journeyman Electrician Exam may be done by visiting the website of the state's testing center, or by a phone call to the testing state. If you need any special accommodations—for example, due to a disability—you can also request this while coordinating with the testing center about your schedule.

How to Prepare for the Journeyman Electrician Exam

Exam preparation goes beyond studying the NEC and practicing electrical calculations. Several experienced apprentices still fail to pass the exam because they do not know the right way to prepare for it.

As a guide, here are some valuable tips that you should apply while preparing for your Journeyman Electrician Exam:

- Gain the support of your family, friends, employer, and co-workers. Preparing for the exam will require you to spend around seven to fourteen hours per week. This study period can last up to six months so you would greatly benefit from the understanding and encouragement of the people around you.

- Establish and follow a consistent schedule every day. You cannot spend the whole day studying for the exam. Instead, you must plan and manage your time well so that you can still handle the other important aspects of your life, such as doing your work, having meals, spending quality time with your loved ones, while preparing for the exam.

> "Willpower is human electricity. You have enough of this electricity generated in you to achieve the greatest things in life if you will keep the current on."
>
> Elsie Lincoln Benedict

- Learn how to manage your stress level.
  Stress management exercises may be done before, during, and after studying for the exam. Simple activities such as doing push-ups,

walking around, or taking deep breaths can do wonders in relaxing both the body and mind. If you feel pain in your neck, shoulders, or back while studying, take a pause and do your stress-relieving exercises for a few minutes or until you feel the tension leaving your body.

- Organize the essentials for the exam.
  Being prepared for the exam does not only mean going through the topics that will be covered. You must also take the time to gather the things that you would likely need during the exam, such as pencils, paper, calculator, folders, and your notes. By doing so ahead of time, you can focus more on answering the questions rather than figuring out where you can do your calculations during the exam.

Some people who have undergone the licensing exam still failed to pass even though they had ample preparation for it. Why?

One of the most common reasons is that they didn't know good test-taking strategies. Below are some tips that can help you achieve the best scores possible during the exam itself.

- Relax.
  Though it sounds easier said than done, staying relaxed during this important exam is one of the keys to passing it. Often, stress makes people forget about what they have studied before. It can also lead to confusion and a lack of focus. Therefore, you must make it a point to keep calm and stay comfortable during the exam. If you feel like you are starting to feel stressed, stop for a bit and do any of your preferred quick relaxation exercises, especially the ones that worked well for you while you were preparing for the exam.

> **Quick Tip!**
> Underline keywords of the question to help you focus while searching for the answer in the code, or while doing your calculations.

- Pay careful attention to each question.
  Read through the entire question before looking up the answer in the Code, or starting your calculations. Missing out on an important word in the question could lead you to either a wrong answer or wasted time.

- Practice the process of elimination.

Since the exam provides multiple choices for each item, there would be options that can be easily eliminated because they are completely outside of the topic of the question, or they sound illogical immediately. Cross out those choices temporarily, and prioritize the options that sound like they could be the correct answer instead.

- Skip questions that are difficult to answer.
  Don't get stuck on a question. You are not required to answer the exam in the order that it is presented. Questions that are too difficult to answer can be skipped for the time being so that you would have enough time and momentum to answer the easy ones first. After your first run through the exam, you can go back to the questions you have skipped, and perhaps the mere act of answering the other easier questions has also helped jog your memory on how the harder questions should be answered.

- Review your answers.
  After answering all or almost all the questions, go through each item again. Look for probable errors—such as marking "b" when you intend to answer "c" or placing the answer for item no. 31 on the spot for no. 30 instead. Avoid changing your answers unless you are completely certain that doing so would correct a wrong selection you have made earlier. Sometimes, the first choice you have made is the right, and doubting yourself during the review could cause you to lose a point.

How to Use the Index

Using the Index for the Journeyman Electrician Exam is one of two widely used methods to look for the definitions, requirements, exceptions, and tables within the NEC.

The topics and keywords under the Index are arranged alphabetically, however, unlike the traditional Index of other books, the NEC Index will point you to the article, part, section, table, or appendix where the said topic or keyword can be found. Inexperienced Code users find this aspect of the Index to be confusing and tedious. Such complaints typically stem from the lack of mastery over the terms, theories, and practices of doing electrical works.

If you do not have enough experience in using the Code Book at this point, you might arrive at the same conclusion. However, don't give up because the Index is one of the most indispensable tools that you can use to pass the licensing exam.

Over time, you will be familiarized with the contents of the NEC, including the Index. Furthermore, you can make things a lot easier if you would customize your Code Book according to how you look up, process, and retain information in your head.

Some of the most effective techniques on using the Index involve highlighting the most frequently used keywords, and placing page tabs on the pages that you normally need as reference. You will learn more about how to use the

> "If you do not have enough experience in using the Code Book at this point, you might arrive at the same conclusion. However, don't give up because the Index is one of the most indispensable tools that you can use to pass the licensing exam."

Index to search for specific Code information in Chapter 4 of this book.

Trying to take any licensing exam without careful preparation is a total waste of time, effort, and money. Don't assume that you can pass with just mere luck on your side. Make the most out of the resources that you have on hand. Take classes, attend seminars, and pay attention to the lessons from your supervising master electrician.

Spend time studying and truly understanding the NEC and what it can do for you. Go through its content little by little if you feel overwhelmed by its comprehensiveness or technicality.

Remember to answer the practice questions in this book. The respective answer keys can be found below each set of questions so that you can better assess your strong and weak points for each topic. Take note of the mistakes you made so that you can refocus your studies and address them immediately.

As a final tip, set aside at least one hour for your self-study each day. By doing so, you will establish good study habits that will not only prevent you from feeling burned out due to extended hours of studying—it will also help you retain more information in the long run.

Now that you have a better idea of what it takes to become a licensed journeyman electrician, let's proceed to the next chapter, which discusses the definition, history, formula, and applications of Ohm's Law.

Chapter 2 – Ohm's Law

Anyone who has studied the fundamental laws of physics knows Ohm's Law. Its application may be observed in day-to-day life since the electric current is necessary to power many of the essential home appliances or work equipment. Through the guidance of Ohm's Law, designers and engineers can determine the right amount of electric current needed to power up their respective works.

Given its significance, you need to learn the formula and applications of Ohm's Law as part of your preparation for the Journeyman Electrician Exam. This chapter covers the basics of Ohm's Law, as well as a brief look at its history and a breakdown of the Ohm's Law pyramid. To test your understanding of its principles and formula, please answer the 10 practice questions at the end of this chapter.

What is Ohm's Law?

Ohm's Law explains how electric current, voltage, and electrical resistance are related and how they interact with one another in an electric circuit.

In simple terms:

- Electric current (I) is directly proportional to voltage (E). This means an increase in electric current also increases the voltage.
- Electrical resistance (R) does not depend on either the electric current or the voltage. Therefore, in this relationship, the value of resistance is constant.

If expressed in a mathematical equation:

$$I = \frac{E}{R}$$

Take note that these relationships exist as long as physical condition and temperature are constant. Moreover, these relationships allow you to determine the value of a component as long as you know the value of the two other components.

To better explain Ohm's Law, many use the water flow analogy. Imagine a stream of water flowing through a pipe. If you increase the water pressure, more water will pass through and come out of the pipe. In this scenario, there is no change in the material composition of the pipe so water flow is only affected when there is a change in water pressure.

When you apply this to electricity, the water flowing through the pipe is similar to the uninterrupted flow of free electrons through a conductor. This is the electric current. It is measured in terms of Amperes or amps (A).

Increasing the water pressure reflects how voltage affects the current. The number of volts (V) refers to the amount of potential energy that exists between two points. Therefore, the movement of free electrons depends on how high or low the voltage is.

The lack of change of water flow when the pressure remains the same can be likened to how the material used for the conductor in an electric circuit affects the current. Free electrons move with a certain degree of opposition. The friction caused by the material of the conductor determines the electrical resistance of the circuit. Ohm had introduced this phenomenon through his works the measure of electrical resistance—ohms or Ω—was named after him.

To summarize:

	Brief Definition	Symbol	Unit of Measure
Current	The flow rate of free electrons	I	Ampere or amp (A)
Voltage	The driving force behind the flow of free electrons	E	Volt (V)
Resistance	The opposition to the flow of free electrons	R	Ohm (Ω)

The History of Ohm's Law

Georg Ohm first presented the results of his work on electrical resistance in 1827 through his book entitled "Die Galvanische Kette, Mathematisch Bearbeitet" (The Galvanic Circuit Investigated Mathematically). While Ohm's Law continues to be widely accepted today, its introduction was met with disbelief and criticism by the academic and scientific community at the time.

Many believe that this harsh reception was influenced by the following:

- Martin Ohm—Georg's younger brother and mathematician—was a critic of the educational system in Germany.
- Back then, the guiding philosophy of many German scientists was against conducting experiments to better understand nature. For them, scientific truths can be obtained by simple reasoning and deduction because nature is in order already.

Because of these, Ohm did not gain recognition for his work until the 1840s, when he received the Copley Medal from The Royal Society of London. To this day, Ohm's Law is still aligned with recent scientific theories on electricity and electromagnetism.

Breaking Down the Ohm's Law Pyramid

Another way to illustrate Ohm's Law is through the pyramid below:

Interesting Fact

Electrical resistance cannot be measured while the circuit is in operation. Rather than powering down the circuit just to determine the resistance, an electrician can just divide the voltage by the current to obtain the answer.

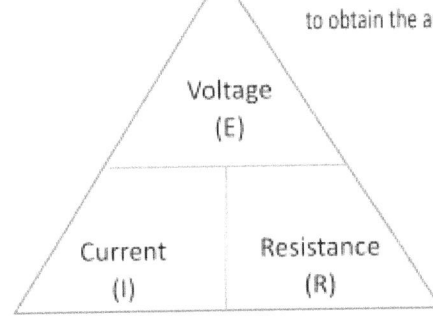

This pyramid contains three formulas that you can use to determine the current, voltage, or resistance in an electrical circuit.

- $Current\ (I) = \frac{Voltage\ (E)}{Resistance\ (R)}$
- $Resistance\ (R) = \frac{Voltage\ (E)}{Current\ (I)}$
- $Voltage\ (E) = Current\ (I) * Resistance\ (R)$

As mentioned earlier, knowing any two of the said values will allow you to compute the value of the third. To better explain how this works, picture in your head a simple series circuit that is made of one lightbulb and one battery. The lightbulb serves as the resistance while the battery is the single source of voltage.

- Scenario 1: You know the voltage and resistance but not the current. If the battery has a voltage of 12 volts and the lightbulb has a resistance of 3 ohms, what is the current in this circuit?
  Using the formula $I = \frac{E}{R}$

$$I = \frac{12\,V}{3\,\Omega}$$

$$I = 4\,A$$

The current of this simple series circuit is 4 amperes.

- Scenario 2: You know the voltage and current but not the resistance.
  If the battery has a voltage of 24 volts and the current is 3 amperes, what is the resistance that is created by the lightbulb?
  Using the formula $R = \frac{E}{I}$

$$R = \frac{24\,V}{3\,A}$$

$$R = 8\,\Omega$$

The lightbulb has a resistance value of 8 ohms.

- Scenario 3: You know the current and the resistance but not the voltage.
  If the current of the circuit is 5 amps and the lightbulb has a resistance value of 6 ohms, what is the voltage of the battery?
  Using the formula $E = I * R$

$$E = 5\,A * 6\,\Omega$$

$$E = 30\,V$$

The battery has a voltage of 30 volts.

To gauge your understanding of Ohm's Law and these formulas, try answering the practice questions in the following section of this chapter.

Practice Questions: Ohm's Law

Instructions: Select the best answer from the given choices.

1. If the current flowing through a circuit is 5 amps and the resistance value of the material is 8 ohms, calculate the voltage for this circuit.
    a. 13 volts
    b. 3 volts
    c. 40 volts
    d. 1.6 volts

2. Ohm's Law states that resistance is directly proportional to voltage.
    a. True
    b. False
3. Calculate the value of resistance if the battery source is 12 volts and the current is 6 amps.
    a. 2 ohms
    b. 6 ohms
    c. 18 ohms
    d. 72 ohms
4. What will happen to the current flowing through an electric circuit if the wire resistance is doubled while the voltage is decreased by 50%?
    a. The current will be increased by 25%
    b. The current will be increased by 75%
    c. The current will be reduced by 25%.
    d. The current will be reduced by 75%
5. What is the current flowing through a circuit that has a 2-ohm resistor and a 10-volt battery?
    a. 20 amps
    b. 12 amps
    c. 5 amps
    d. 0.5 amps
6. Ohm's Law is not affected even if there is a variation of temperature in the electrical circuit.
    a. True
    b. False
7. Which of the following variations of Ohm's Law is accurate?
    a. $E = I * R$
    b. $I = \frac{R}{E}$
    c. $R = \frac{V}{E}$
    d. $I = E * R$
8. A 20-volt battery is connected to a 5-ohm lightbulb. How much current is flowing through this circuit?
    a. 4 amps
    b. 5 amps
    c. 25 amps
    d. 100 amps
9. A refrigerator is connected to a 20 _____ circuit breaker so that the device will be triggered if excessive _____ flows through the breaker.

a. volt, voltage
b. amp, resistance
c. ohm, voltage
d. amp, current

10. What is the voltage of a battery if the current flowing through the circuit is 25 amps and its resistance value is 4 ohms?
    a. 25 volts
    b. 50 volts
    c. 100 volts
    d. 200 volts

Answer Key: Ohm's Law

1. c. 40 volts

   To get the answer, use the formula for voltage: $E = I * R$ (where E = voltage, I = current, and R = resistance)

   $E = 5\ amps * 8\ ohms$

   $E = 40\ volts$

2. b. False

   Ohm's Law states that current—not resistance—is directly proportional to voltage.

3. a. 2 ohms

   Compute the resistance using this formula: $R = \frac{E}{I}$ (where R = resistance, E = voltage, and I = current)

   $R = \frac{12\ volts}{6\ amps}$

   $R = 2\ ohms$

4. d. The current will be reduced by 75%.

   To figure out the right answer, let's assume that the voltage is 50 volts and the resistance value is 25 ohms. Given these, the electric current is 2 amps.

If the voltage would be decreased by half, it would become 25 volts. Doubling the resistance value means that it would be 50 ohms. Based on these adjustments, the new current is 0.5 amps.

To solve for how much percentage the current had decreased, just apply this formula:

$$Percentage\ Decreased = 100\% - (\frac{New\ Current}{Old\ Current} * 100\%)$$

$$Percentage\ Decreased = 100\% - (0.25 * 100\%)$$

$$Percentage\ Decreased = 75\%$$

5. c. 5 amps
   Use this formula to solve for the current flow in the given circuit: $I = \frac{E}{R}$
   (where I = current, E = voltage, and R = resistance)
   $$I = \frac{10\ volts}{2\ ohms}$$
   $$I = 5\ amps$$

6. b. False
   As stated earlier, the relationships of current, voltage, and resistance that are defined in Ohm's Law will hold as long as there is no change in the physical condition or temperature.

7. a. $E = I \times R$
   Here are the correct formulas that are based on Ohm's
   - $I = \frac{E}{R}$
   - $E = I * R$
   - $R = \frac{E}{I}$

   Of the four choices, only the formula indicated under choice "a" is accurate.

8. a. 4 amps
   To determine the current flow, apply this formula: $I = \frac{E}{R}$ (where I = current, E = voltage, and R = resistance)
   $$I = \frac{20\ volts}{5\ ohms}$$
   $$I = 4\ amps$$

9. d. amp, current

   A circuit breaker is designed to keep an electric circuit from being damaged due to excessive current flow due to various factors, like a short circuit or an overload. Therefore, a 20-amp circuit breaker will be set off if the current flow exceeds its limit.

10. c. 100 volts

    Use this formula to solve for the battery's voltage: $E = I * R$ (where E = voltage, I = current, and R = resistance)

$E = 25\ amps * 4\ ohms$

$E = 100\ volts$

Chapter 3 – Electrical Theory

To make sense of rules and guidelines stated in the NEC, you must have pre-existing knowledge of the basic electrical laws, and concepts. Since you are planning to take the Journeyman Electrician Exam, you have likely gained a practical understanding of these concepts during your apprenticeship. Still, it would be in your best interest to go through the basics again to refresh your memory and solidify the foundation of your technical skills as an electrician.

This chapter is designed to help you remember the important laws and concepts that you should know to understand the NEC, pass the licensing exam, and complete electrical works that are well-designed and safe to use.

The Three Primary Forces

All electrical circuits are controlled by three primary forces: current, voltage, and impedance. If you had gone through the previous chapter of this book, then you have already encountered two of these terms because Ohm's Law defines and explains the relationships that exist among the fundamental electrical forces. Take note that many people assume that impedance and resistance are the same. However, as you will learn in this chapter, there are critical differences between the two concepts.

> "Faith is like electricity. You can't see it, but you can see its light shining on you."
>
> — Antoni Zygmund

Current

Current refers to the flow of free electrons through a conductor in an electrical circuit. In mathematical formulas, it is symbolized with the capitalized letter "I" because its full technical name is "Intensity of Current Flow."

In electricity, the current is measured in terms of amperes or amps (symbolized by the capital letter "A"). Each ampere is equal to 6.25×10^{23} electrons per second. This force is typically likened to the flow of water, which may be measured by the number of gallons per minute. If applied in the context of electricity, this would mean that a circuit where the current flow is 20A has four times more electrons flowing through its conductor compared to a circuit that has a current flow of 5A.

Voltage

This is the primary force that is responsible for the movement of current in an electrical circuit. Some represent this with the capitalized letter "V", but based on its scientific name "Electromotive Force", the more typical symbol for voltage is the capital letter "E". The latter is better suited for mathematical computations since it is distinct from the symbol for volts (V)—the standard unit of measure for voltage.

A volt refers to the amount of voltage or electromotive force needed to trigger 1 amp of current to flow through a material that has a resistance value of 1 ohm. This means that the higher the voltage is, the higher the current flow will be in a given electrical circuit.

Impedance

This refers to the total opposing force against the flow of free electrons in an alternating current (AC) circuit. In formulas, this force is represented by the capital letter "Z".

Much like resistance, it is measured in terms of ohms, which is symbolized by the Greek letter "Ω" (omega). An ohm is equivalent to the amount of opposition of a conductor in a circuit that has a current flow of 1 amp and a potential difference of 1 volt.

One way to compute the impedance in a circuit is by applying the principles of Ohm's Law. As such, the basic formula for impedance is: $Z = \frac{E}{I}$

> Where:
>
> > Z = impedance
> > E = voltage
> > I = current

In electrical works and mathematical problems, resistance is more commonly used than impedance. However, of the two concepts, impedance can better describe the flow of electricity through a circuit than resistance. Why?

Using resistance to describe the opposing force is acceptable if the circuit involved has no reactance. In reality, though, almost all modern electrical circuits—AC circuits, in particular, have some degree of reactance. Therefore,

> *"In electrical works and mathematical problems, resistance is more commonly used than impedance. However, of the two concepts, impedance can better describe the flow of electricity through a circuit than resistance."*

you will get a more accurate measure of how much a material can restrict electrical flow by using impedance rather than resistance.

When calculating impedance, you must first remember that the reactance in AC circuits comes from two sources: the magnetic coils and the capacitors. Magnetic coils cause inductive reactance, while the latter causes capacitive reactance. You will learn more about these terms in the succeeding section.

Given these, the general formula for impedance is: $Z = \sqrt{R^2 + (X_L - X_C)^2}$

Where:

Z = impedance
R = resistance
X_L = inductive reactance
X_C = capacitive reactance

You can use this formula for any type of electrical circuit, especially when resistance, inductive reactance, and capacitive reactance are all present.

If only resistance and inductive reactance are present, then you can modify the general formula to this: $Z = \sqrt{R^2 + X_L^2}$

Conversely, if only resistance and capacitive reactance are present, then the formula for impedance should be: $Z = \sqrt{R^2 + X_C^2}$

Reactance

As mentioned earlier, reactance can only be observed in AC circuits. It is represented by the capitalized letter "X" in mathematical formulas. Meanwhile, the two types of reactance—inductive and capacitive—are symbolized in formulas by "X_L" and "X_C" respectively.

Inductive Reactance

This refers to the type of resistance caused by wire coils, especially magnetic ones. Also known as inductors, common examples of these wire coils are motors and transformers.

Inductive reactance opposes a change in current flowing through a circuit. As a result, when the voltage starts to increase, the current flow does not immediately increase—instead, it lags behind the voltage. The exact amount of lag depends on how much inductive reactance there is in the electrical circuit. For example, if the circuit is 100% inductive only, there will be a lag of 90 degrees.

To calculate the inductive reactance, just apply this formula: $X_L = 2\pi FL$

Where:

X_L = inductive reactance

F = frequency

L = inductance

> **Remember!**
>
> The primary difference between AC and DC can be observed in the direction of the current flow.

The unit of measurement for frequency is "hertz" (Hz) while inductance is measured in terms of "henry" (H). Similar to impedance and resistance, inductive reactance is measured in ohms (Ω). As depicted in the formula, the higher the frequency is, the higher the amount of inductive reactance there will be, too.

Capacitive Reactance

This type of reactance occurs because capacitors oppose changes in voltage. It causes the current to be in the lead of the voltage in an electrical circuit. Given this, you can typically observe capacitors being used in circuits to correct the current lag that happens in inductive circuits.

What is a capacitor? This electrical device is made of two slightly separated metal plates or foil that can conduct electricity. Since the two parts are not connected electrically, it can only store energy but it does not allow the flow of electrons from one metal surface to the other.

If used in a DC (direct current) circuit, a capacitor will store electrons for a short while, thus allowing a small amount of current to flow. However, once the capacitor becomes full of energy, the current flow will stop because the electrical circuit is not complete.

In comparison, a capacitor used in an AC circuit will store electrons during the first alternation. Once the direction of the current reverses, the currently stored electrons will be released and the capacitor will store other electrons instead. This gives the capacitor the ability to keep the current flowing in the circuit as it continually stores and releases electrons in time with changes in the direction of the current.

In a completely capacitive circuit, the current leads the voltage by 90 degrees. To calculate the capacitive reactance in a circuit, use this formula: $X_C = \frac{1}{2\pi FC}$

Where:

X_C = capacitive reactance
F = frequency
C = capacitance

Capacitance is measured in terms of farads. One farad is equivalent to the capacitance that is needed to store 6.25 x 10^{23} (1 coulomb) of electrons in a circuit that has an electrical pressure of 1 volt. However, because of the significantly high amount of capacitance caused by this storage, the more common units of measure used for capacitive reactance are either microfarads or picofarads.

Did You Know That...

Electric eels can produce up to 500 volts of electric shocks. This is their primary self-defense against potential predators, but they can also use these electric shocks to hunt for food.

Practice Questions: Reactance
Instructions: Select the best answer from the given choices.

1. What is the inductive reactance of an AC circuit that has an inductance value of 0.3H and a frequency of 60Hz?
    a. 180.30 ohms
    b. 113.04 ohms
    c. 60.3 ohms
    d. 0.005 ohms
2. Calculate the capacitive reactance if the frequency is at 30Hz and a 120-microfarad capacitor (1 farad = 1,000,000 microfarads) is used for the circuit.
    a. 44.23 ohms

b. 60.32 ohms
   c. 75.12 ohms
   d. 80.54 ohms
3. What is the frequency of a 150H inductor to have an inductive reactance of 5,000Ω?
   a. 10.34 hertz
   b. 8.45 hertz
   c. 5.31 hertz
   d. 3.67 hertz
4. Find out the voltage of a circuit that has a current value of 4.8A and a capacitive reactance of 25Ω.
   a. 240 volts
   b. 120 volts
   c. 60 volts
   d. 30 volts
5. If a coil with an inductance value of 0.8H is connected to a 240-volt circuit that has a frequency of 20Hz, how much electric current is flowing in that circuit?
   a. 2.39 amperes
   b. 5.14 amperes
   c. 8.23 amperes
   d. 12.39 amperes

Answer Key: Reactance
1. b. 113.04 ohms
   To get this answer, simply apply the formula for inductive reactance:
   $X_L = 2\pi FL$ (where X_L = inductive reactive, F = frequency, and L = inductance)
   $X_L = 2 * 3.14 * 60\ hertz * 0.3\ henry$
   $X_L = 113.04\ ohms$

2. a. 44.23 ohms
   Use the formula for capacitive reactance to get the answer.
   $X_C = \frac{1}{2\pi FC}$ (where X_C = capacitive reactance, F = frequency, and C = capacitance)
   $X_C = \frac{1{,}000{,}000}{2 * 3.14 * 30 * 120\ microfarads}$

X_C = 44.23 ohms

3. c. 5.31 hertz
   Given that the formula for inductive reactive is $X_L = 2\pi FL$ (where X_L = inductive reactive, F = frequency, and L = inductance, you may find out the frequency by doing some algebraic manipulation, as demonstrated below:
   5,000 ohms = 2πF * 150 henrys
   $F = \dfrac{5{,}000 \; ohms}{2 * 3.14 * 150 \; henrys}$
   F = 5.31 hertz

4. b. 120 volts
   To compute the voltage, you need to apply the Ohm's Law formula for voltage, but remember to substitute the value of resistance with the capacitive reactance given in the question.
   $E = IX_C$ (where E = voltage, I = current, and X_C = capacitive reactance)
   $E = 4.8 \; amperes * 25 \; ohms$
   E = 120 volts

5. a. 2.39 amperes
   Again, this question is testing your understanding of reactance and Ohm's Law. To determine the current, you need to calculate the inductive reactance first.
   $X_L = 2\pi FL$ (where X_L = inductive reactive, F = frequency, and L = inductance)
   $X_L = 2 * 3.14 * 20 \; hertz * 0.8 \; henry$
   $X_L = 100.48 \; ohms$
   Next, apply the Ohm's Law formula for electric current.
   $I = \dfrac{E}{R}$ (where I = current, E = voltage, and R = resistance
   However, in this case, you can substitute resistance with inductive reactance. Therefore, your computation should look like this:
   $I = \dfrac{E}{X_L}$ (where X_L = inductive reactance)
   $I = \dfrac{240 \; volts}{100.48 \; ohms}$
   I = 2.39 amperes

Electric Power

By now, you are familiar with the definitions and roles of current and voltage in an electrical circuit. What happens though if these two interact?

The answer: electric power.

In our day-to-day lives, the applications of electric power can be observed in almost every aspect. Many of the appliances in your home rely on electric power to run and perform their respective functions. Electric power is also present in the equipment at your workplaces, such as computers and the overhead lights. On an industrial level, massive electric power grids are necessary to ensure the steady supply of electricity to residential, commercial, and public properties.

Simply speaking, electric power is the amount of work performed per unit of time. It is measured in terms of watts so when you hear someone speak of a device's wattage, it is about the electric power it needs to operate.

> **Did You Know That...**
>
> The biggest source of electricity remains to be coal. To produce electric power, burning coal is needed to heat the furnaces that are used to boil water. The steam generated by this process is necessary to spin the large turbines of generators.

In an equation, electric power is represented by the capitalized letter "P".

Calculating this depends on the information available to you. For example, if you know the voltage and current flow, then you may apply this formula:

$$P = E * I$$

Where:

P = electric power
E = voltage
I = current

Based on this equation, voltage is the degree of strength needed to move the electric charge, while the current is the amount of electric charge that is being moved. Variations of this formula for electric power if you consider the resistance value of the circuit and the time required to move the charge. In this case, the formula becomes:

$$P = E * I = I^2 * R = \frac{E^2}{R}$$

Where:

- P = electric power
- I = current
- R = resistance
- E = voltage

On the other hand, if you know the amount of work needed to move 1 coulomb through 1-volt potential difference, you may compute the electric power as long as you also know the time it takes to conduct that work. In the context of electricity, work is typically measured in Joules, and it is equivalent to 1 watt-second.

Given these variables, the formula for electric power is:

$$P = \frac{W}{t}$$

Where:

- P = electric power
- W = work
- t = time

Take note that for this equation, time should be in terms of seconds.

Given that current is the product of electric charge and voltage, another formula for electric power is:

$$P = \frac{Q * V}{t}$$

Where:

- P = electric power
- Q = electric charge
- V = voltage
- t = time

Your understanding of electric power is not going to be comprehensive if you do not learn about the differences between reactive power, real power, and apparent power.

Reactive Power

This type is also known as the "phantom power" because reactive loads give a false impression that they dissipate power. However, there is no power loss in reality. It only appears so when current is drawn and voltage is dropped by the loads.

Because it is not electric power in the technical sense, the unit of measure for reactive power is VAR (volt-amps-reactive). In equations, this type is symbolized by the capitalized letter "Q".

To compute the reactive power, use either of the formulas below, depending on the information you have.

$$\text{Option 1: } Q = \frac{E^2}{X}$$

Where:

- Q = reactive power
- E = voltage
- X = reactance

$$\text{Option 2: } Q = I^2 * X$$

Where:

- Q = reactive power
- I = current
- X = reactance

Real Power

Also referred to as "true" power, this is the actual amount of electric power being used in a given circuit. It shares the symbol, capital letter "P", with electric power. Moreover, real power is measured in terms of watts.

Given these, you need to apply the same formula as the one used for calculating electric power: $P = I^2 * R = \frac{E^2}{R}$

Where:

- P = electric power
- I = current

R = resistance
E = voltage

Because of its relatively complicated nature, a specialized wattmeter has to be used to take the readings of the voltage and current. These readings will then be averaged to determine the real power. A reactive power meter may also be used to measure a circuit's real power.

Apparent Power

When you put together the reactive power and real power, you will get the apparent power of a circuit. The primary defining characteristic of this type is that it reflects the product of voltage and ampere in a given electric circuit, however, it does not take into account the phase angle or variance between the two factors.

Apparent power is a function of the total impedance in a circuit. Therefore, you may use the value of impedance to compute the circuit's apparent power.

In an equation, apparent power is symbolized by the capital letter "S". Its unit of measure is Volt-Amp (VA). To calculate this, use the following any of the following formulas based on the values that have been specified about the circuit:

$$\text{Option 1: } S = I^2 * Z$$

Where:

S = apparent power
I = current
Z = impedance

$$\text{Option 2: } S = I * E$$

Where:

S = apparent power
I = current
E = voltage

Apparent power can be measured with the use of common electrician tools, such as an ammeter or a voltmeter. This is possible because as the name implies, it is the kind of power that is immediately perceptible.

How do the three relate to one another in an electric circuit?

- In a reactive circuit, apparent power is greater than real power. The ratio between the two refers to the concept called the power factor. You will learn more about the power factor in the latter part of this chapter.
- If the power factor is 1.0, then no difference exists between the real power and apparent power of the circuit. Such cases are referred to as "unity."
- In a circuit that has absolutely no reactance, the values of real power and apparent power are the same. However, everything becomes more complicated than this when the movements of the current and the voltage become out of phase with one another.

Practice Questions: Electric Power

Instructions: Select the best answer from the given choices.

1. A 12-volt battery is connected to a circuit with a current flow of 0.25 amps. What is the electric power in this circuit?
    a. 3 watts
    b. 6 watts
    c. 10 watts
    d. 12 watts
2. Electrician Mark inspects a circuit before conducting his work. His measurement shows that the potential difference is 20V while the electric power is 30W. The total amount of electric charge is 350 C. How much time is needed for the charge to flow through the given circuit?
    a. 300.57 seconds
    b. 275.65 seconds
    c. 233.33 seconds
    d. 201.48 seconds
3. Which of the following statements about apparent power is false?
    a. You can measure the apparent power in an electric circuit through the use of an ammeter.
    b. If there is an equal amount of real power and apparent power, then the power factor ratio is 1.0.
    c. The unit of measure for apparent power is volt-amps (VA).
    d. Apparent power is synonymous with electric power.

4. When the power factor is 1.0, the real power of a circuit is greater than its apparent power.
   a. True
   b. False
5. Real power can be measured using which of the following instruments?
   a. Ammeter
   b. Voltmeter
   c. Wattmeter
   d. All of the above

Answer Key: Electric Power

1. a. 3 watts

   To solve for electric power in the given circuit, use this formula: $P = EI$ (where P = electric power, E = voltage, and I = current)

   $P = 12\ volts * 0.25\ amps$

   $P = 3\ watts$

2. c. 233.33 seconds

   Electrician Mark should derive the formula for the time from this equation: $P = \frac{QV}{t}$ (where P = electric power, Q = electric charge, V = voltage, t = time)

   $30\ watts = \frac{350\ coulombs * 20\ volts}{t}$

   $t = \frac{350\ coulombs * 20\ volts}{30\ watts}$

   $t = 233.33\ seconds$

3. d. Apparent power is synonymous with electric power.
   This is inaccurate because it is the real power that is the same as electric power. Apparent power is the combined amount of real power and reactive power of a circuit.

4. b. False

A power factor of 1.0 indicates that the real power and apparent power of the circuit are of equal value.

5. c. wattmeter
   A wattmeter is used to take the readings of the current and voltage in a circuit. These readings will then be used to calculate the real power. On the other hand, ammeters and voltmeters are used to measure the apparent power.

Electric Charge

Electric charge refers to the physical property of sub-atomic particles that makes them respond to a force if placed in a field that is electrically, magnetically, or electromagnetically charged.

In an equation, electric charge is represented by the capital letter "Q", while its standard unit of measure is the coulomb (C). One coulomb is equal to the charge quantity that is moved in 1 second. Other ways to express electric charge are through ampere-hour (Ah) or faraday (F).

To compute for electric charge, use the following formula: $Q = I * t$

> Where:
>
> > Q = electric charge
> > I = current
> > t = time

There are two types of electric charge: positive (+) charge and negative (-) charge.

- Positive Charge
  If an object has more protons than electrons, then it is positively charged.
- Negative Charge
  A negatively charged object has a greater number of electrons than protons.

When placed near each other, two protons or two electrons would repel each other. On the other hand, the opposite charges of a proton and an electron cause them to become attracted to each other.

What if there is an equal number of protons and electrons? The charges of each subatomic particle would cancel one another, thereby making the object neutral.

A neutral object may be charged through 3 different methods:

- Charging by Friction
  Rubbing two objects against each other will cause Object A to lose electrons to Object B. As a result, Object A becomes positively charged, while the newly gained electrons turn the charge of Object B to negative. In this method, the electrical charges of both objects are changed through friction.

  A common example of charging via friction—or also known as the triboelectric charging process—is fixing your hair with the use of a plastic comb. After doing so, the comb will gain the ability to attract small and light materials, such as tiny bits of paper.

- Charging by Conduction
  If you place an uncharged object against a charged object, a transfer of electrons may occur between the two. This occurs because the charged object has too many electrons compared to protons.

  Because of the proximity of the uncharged object, an arc of electricity forms between the two as the latter will attempt to stabilize its charge by discharging the extra electrons. Since this method requires physical contact to work, it is also known as charging by contact.

  > **Take Note!**
  >
  > Charging by friction occurs because the two objects are made of different materials. The object that has weaker electron bonds will lose the electrons when it is rubbed against the other object with stronger electron bonds.

  Let's go over this example to better understand how this works:
  - In this scenario, there are two metal objects—one is uncharged, while the

other is negatively charged. Both objects have similar properties, and both are placed on an insulated stand.
- When you bring the two objects close to each other—without letting either of them interact with anything else—you will observe a separation of charge occurring in the uncharged object. Its electrons are repelled to the side away from the negatively charged object, while its protons remain or are pulled closer towards the negatively charged object.
- When physical contact is made between the two objects, some of the electrons from the negatively charged object will move towards the uncharged object. Because the electrons were already repelling each other in the first object, they will grab the opportunity to move further away from each other by transferring into the uncharged object.
- When you pull away from the two objects from one another, the negatively charged object will have fewer electrons in it. On the other hand, the formerly uncharged object will now be negatively charged, too.

The same phenomenon will happen if a positively charged rod made contact with an uncharged metal ball. However, in this case, the neutral metal ball will transfer its electrons to the rod.

As you may have noticed, this is why some materials are better at conducting electricity while others serve as insulators. Conductors allow the easy movement of electric charges, while insulators inhibit such movements.

- Charging by Induction
This method requires no physical contact between the two objects. Like conduction, it involves bringing an uncharged object near a charged object. However, in this case, the two objects do not touch the surface of one another, and yet a transfer of electrons still occurs between the two.

How is this possible?

To make this work, you need to use a grounding wire. This can be any type of conductor that will connect the neutral object to the ground. The ground can gain or release electrons depending on the scenario.

As a way to better illustrate how charging by induction works, take a look at the example below:
- o If the negatively charged object is brought near the grounded neutral object, then the electrons of the latter will be pushed away. As a result, the said electrons will move down the grounding wire.
- o To ensure that the neutral object will become and continue to be positively charged, you must cut the grounding wire while the negatively charged object is still nearby. By doing so, you are effectively preventing the electrons from traveling back up to the grounded object. If that occurs, then the charge of the object would revert to its neutral state.
- o When you remove the negatively charged object, the neutral object will become positively charged.

Similar subatomic behaviors will be observed if you place a positively charged object near a grounding wire. In this scenario, the electrons will travel towards the object, thereby changing the electric charge of the neutral object to negative.

Practice Questions: Electric Charge
Instructions: Select the best answer from the given choices.

1. Ben polishes a glass rod with the use of silk cloth. As a result, the glass rod becomes positively charged. Given this, which of the following statements is true?
   a. The silk cloth has gained a positive charge.
   b. The silk cloth has gained a negative charge.
   c. The silk cloth has remained neutral.

Interesting Fact

Electricity moves at the speed of light—well, almost! Electric current flows at 186,000 kilometers per second.

    d. The silk cloth can either be positively or negatively charged.
2. A circuit has a current value of 2A. How much electric charge will pass through a point within this circuit in 10 seconds?
    a. 20 coulombs
    b. 12 coulombs
    c. 8 coulombs
    d. 5 coulombs
3. A rod with a negative charge has been brought near a set of two metal balls that are in physical contact with each other but are both insulated from the ground. What will happen to the charge of the metal balls if they will be separated from one another?
    a. The metal ball closed to the rod will become negatively charged, while the other metal ball will have a positive charge.
    b. The metal ball closer to the rod will become positively charged, while the other metal ball will have a negative charge.
    c. The metal balls will become neutral.
    d. None of the above.
4. An electric charge of 180 coulombs passed a point in a circuit in 60 seconds. What is the value of the current flowing through this circuit?
    a. 10,800 amperes
    b. 240 amperes
    c. 120 amperes
    d. 3 amperes
5. How long will it take for an electric charge of 1,000 coulombs to pass a certain point in a circuit that has a current value of 4A?
    a. 4,000 seconds
    b. 1,000 seconds
    c. 250 seconds
    d. 4 seconds

Answer Key: Electric Charge
1. b. The silk cloth has gained a negative charge.
Given that the glass rod had become positively charged after rubbing it with the silk cloth, it means that the object has fewer electrons by the end of it. Therefore, the silk rod acquired electrons during the process, and it had become negatively charged.

2. a. 20 coulombs

> Since the formula for electric charge is Q = It (where Q = electric charge, I = current, and t = time), the computation should be like this:
> Q = 2 amperes * 10 seconds
> Q = 20 coulombs

3. b. The metal ball closer to the rod will become positively charged, while the other metal ball will have a negative charge.
   This scenario demonstrates how charging by induction works. When the rod was brought near one of the metal balls, its negative charge triggers a movement of charges in the metal balls. The metal ball that was further away from the rod would gain more electrons, thus leaving the metal ball closer to the rod as positively charged.

4. d. 3 amperes
   You can find out the answer to this question by making an equation based on the electric charge formula.
   > Q = It (where Q = electric charge, I = current, and t = time)
   > 180 coulombs = I * 60 seconds
   > $I = \frac{180\ coulombs}{60\ seconds}$
   > I = 3 amperes

5. c. 250 seconds
   Again, the formula for time can be derived from how the electric charge is computed.
   > Q = I * t (where Q = electric charge, I = current, and t = time)
   > 1,000 coulombs = 4 amperes * t
   > $t = \frac{1,000\ coulombs}{4\ amperes}$
   > t = 250 seconds

Power Efficiency

In the field of electrical engineering, power efficiency refers to the actual amount of power that had gone to the components versus the total amount of electric power that was drawn from the source. For example, if a power supply has a power efficiency of 50%, then it will need 100 watts of power for its load to receive 50 watts.

Power efficiency is typically expressed in percentage, and it is symbolized by the Greek letter "η" (eta). To determine the power efficiency of an electrical system, apply this formula: $\eta = \frac{P_{out}}{P_{in}} * 100\%$

Where:

η = power efficiency
P_{out} = output power used
P_{in} = input power consumed

Let's take a look at this example to better understand how this formula can be used.

The input power consumed by an electric kettle is 60 watts when it was turned on for 60 seconds. If the total work produced is 3,000 joules, what is the efficiency of the motor?

Before applying the formula, take note that the output power is not directly stated in the question. Instead, you were given the factors needed to calculate power. As such, you need to apply the formula for power first.

$P_{out} = \frac{W}{t}$ (where P_{out} = output power used, W = work, and t = time)

$P_{out} = \frac{3{,}000 \; joules}{60 \; seconds}$

$P_{out} = 50 \; watts$

Now that you have all the components of the formula, proceed to your computation of the kettle's power efficiency.

$\eta = \frac{P_{out}}{P_{in}} * 100\%$

$\eta = \frac{50 \; watts}{60 \; watts} * 100\%$

$\eta = 83.33\%$

The final answer shows that the power efficiency of the electric kettle is 83.33%. Most electrical systems fall within the range of 50 to 99% power efficiency. High power efficiency can be usually observed in systems that use batteries. Low power efficiency may still be improved by tweaking the design of the system or replacing certain components.

> **Did You Know That...**
>
> Heat contributes to the decrease in power efficiency? That's why excessive heat within a given system should be prevented or removed immediately so that the device would operate at its supposed efficiency level. Your appliances at home, for example, might be increasing your electric bills because it forces the air conditioning system to work harder to achieve the desired area temperature.

Practice Questions: Power Efficiency

Instructions: Select the best answer from the given choices.

1. What is the power efficiency of a 3-HP motor (1 mechanical horsepower = 745.7 watts) that draws a current flow of 20A at 120V?
    a. 99.6%
    b. 97.1%
    c. 93.2%
    d. 90.4%
2. In an air conditioning unit, which of the following is not considered waste?
    a. The energy that powers the cooling components of the ACU
    b. The heat that dissipates out of the ACU
    c. The humming sound of a working ACU
    d. None of the above
3. A string of small LED lights wrapped around a Christmas tree emits 10W of light radiation for an input power of 200W. Calculate the power efficiency of the LED lights.
    a. 120%
    b. 50%
    c. 10%
    d. 5%
4. How much is the useful power of a desk lamp that has a power efficiency of 25% when it receives 300W from the electric socket?
    a. 300 watts

    b. 150 watts
    c. 75 watts
    d. 50 watts
5. Which of the following statements is false?
    a. Power efficiency is represented by the Greek letter "η" in equations.
    b. The output power used by an electric kettle with a power efficiency of 85% and draws 100 watts from the wall socket is 85 watts.
    c. Low power efficiency cannot be improved or corrected anymore.
    d. The power efficiency of a hairdryer that requires 1,500 watts of electric power to reach an output of 750 watts is 50%.

Answer Key: Power Efficiency

1. c. 93.2%

    To solve for the power efficiency of the motor, first convert the output power used that is expressed in horsepower to watts. Given that 1HP = 745.7W:

$$Output\ Power\ Consumed = 3 * 745.7$$

$$Output\ Power\ Consumed = 2,237.1\ watts$$

Next, calculate its input power consumed using this formula: $P_{in} = IV$ (where P_{in} = input power consumed, I = current, and V = voltage)

$$P_{in} = 20\ amperes * 120\ volts$$

$$P_{in} = 2,400\ watts$$

Finally, compute the power efficiency by applying this formula:

$$η = \frac{P_{out}}{P_{in}} * 100\%\ (where\ η = power\ efficiency,\ P_{out} = output\ power\ used,\ and\ P_{in} = input\ power\ consumed)$$

$$η = \frac{2,237.1\ watts}{2,400\ watts} * 100\%$$

$$η = 93.2\%$$

2. a. The energy that powers the cooling components of the ACU
   Neither the heat nor the sound generated by an operational ACU contributes to its primary function, which is to cool down the surrounding area. Therefore, the two other choices are considered as wastes.

3. d. 5%
   Use this formula to calculate the power efficiency of the LED lights:
   $$\eta = \frac{P_{out}}{P_{in}} * 100\% \text{ (where } \eta = \text{power efficiency, } P_{out} = \text{output power used, and } P_{in} = \text{input power consumed)}$$
   $$\eta = \frac{10 \text{ watts}}{200 \text{ watts}} * 100\%$$
   $$\eta = 5\%$$

4. c. 75 watts
   To find out the amount of useful power, you may derive the formula for output power used from this: $\eta = \frac{P_{out}}{P_{in}} * 100\%$ *(where η = power efficiency, P_{out} = output power used, and P_{in} = input power consumed)*
   $$25\% = \frac{P_{out}}{300 \text{ watts}} * 100\%$$
   $$P_{out} = 300 \text{ watts} * 0.25$$
   $$P_{out} = 75 \text{ watts}$$

5. c. Low power efficiency cannot be improved or corrected anymore.
   As explained earlier, power efficiency may still be increased by making changes to the design or components of the device or electrical system.

Power Factor

As mentioned earlier, the power factor reflects the relationship between real power and apparent power. Simply speaking, it is the ratio between the amount of power that is used and the amount of power that is being demanded by the system.

Think of a mug full of draft beer. The beer itself may be likened to real power. This is the part that you want to drink. In the context of electricity, this is the power that is doing the actual work.

The beer that contains the beer represents apparent power for this analogy. In most instances, the apparent power is greater than the real power—just like how beer mugs are rarely 100% filled to their brim. Apparent power is also known as the demand of the load

On top of the liquid part of the beer is a layer of foam. This part is similar to the role of reactive power in an electric circuit. It is considered a waste or a loss since the energy it produces does not do any work. Common examples include the heat generated when a motor is running, or the vibration of an electric fan while it is turned on.

> **Take Note!**
>
> Many utility companies ask their customers to pay a so-called demand charge to offset the costs when the electric supply is lower than the demand. Furthermore, utility companies include a surcharge in the billing to customers with known low power factors. Because wasted power can be quite costly, some companies penalize their customers for overusing the supplied power. Correcting the poor power factor ratio will allow you to avoid incurring penalties.

If an electric circuit has completely efficient, then the real power would be equivalent to the apparent power. The reactive power in this case is equal to zero. However, if the apparent power is higher than the real power, then the difference between the two must be considered. AC circuits, for instance, do not have power factors of 1.0 because of the presence of impedance in this electrical system.

To better understand the relationship of impedance with real power and apparent power, imagine a right triangle where the adjacent side is the real power and the hypotenuse is the apparent power.

Meanwhile, the opposite of the triangle signifies the reactive power. The power factor ratio is related to the circuit's impedance because it is equivalent to the cosine of the impedance phase angle. Given this, you may calculate the value of real power, apparent power, or reactive power if you know the length of at least two sides of the power triangle, or if you know the length of one side and the phase angle.

Let's try solving for the power factor using this formula:

$$Power\ Factor = \frac{Real\ Power}{Apparent\ Power}$$

If you would recall from the earlier section about electric power, real power is measured in terms of watts (W), while apparent power is measured in volt-amps (VA) and reactive power is measured in volt-amps-reactive (VAR).

In this scenario, the real power of an electrical system is 120 watts. On the other hand, its apparent power is 170 volt-amps while its reactive power is 119VAR. What is the power factor of this system?

$$Power\ Factor = \frac{120W}{170VA}$$

$$Power\ Factor = 0.71$$

Take note that there is no unit of measure for power factor because ratios do not require a unit of measure.

Learning how the power factor works are important for people who deal with AC circuits. Any system that does not have a power factor of 1.0 indicates that the wiring of the electric circuit will have to higher current flow than what is expected if there is no reactance.

Looking back at the example above, a perfectly efficient system should have been able to dissipate 170W rather than just 120W. Remember, lower power factors mean that the power delivery system is working inefficiently.

Paradoxically speaking, power factor corrections may be performed on poorly performing systems. By adding another load to the system, an equal and opposite amount of reactive power will be drawn, thereby neutralizing the effects of reactance.

For example, since inductive reactance cancels out the capacitive reaction, add a capacitor as an extra load to a parallel circuit. By doing so, the opposing components will bring the value of total impedance to zero—or at least almost to zero.

Let's use the earlier example again and find out how that power factor ratio can be corrected. Since the inductor reactive power is 119 VAR, then you need to determine which capacitor size will generate the right amount of capacitive reactive power to cancel it out. For this example, take note that the voltage is 120 volts and the frequency is 60 hertz.

First, to solve for the reactance, apply this formula:

$$Q = \frac{E^2}{X}$$

Where:

Q = reactive power
E = voltage
X = reactance

From this, we can derive the following formula for reactance:

$$X = \frac{E^2}{Q}$$

$$X = \frac{(120V)^2}{119 VAR}$$

$$X = 121 \Omega$$

Next, let's calculate the capacitance. The basis should be the formula for capacitive reactance:

$$X_C = \frac{1}{2\pi FC}$$

Where:

X_C = capacitive reactance
F = frequency
C = capacitance

Based on this formula, you can solve for the capacitance through this derived formula:

$$C = \frac{1}{2\pi F X_C}$$

$$C = \frac{1}{2*3.14*60*121\Omega}$$

C = 21.93 microfarads

To check how an added capacitor will affect the system, compute again the real power and apparent power but with the one capacitor with a rounded-up value of 22 microfarads as an additional load.

In this scenario, the power factor ratio before the additional capacitor is 0.71. However, with the added 22-microfarad capacitor, the main current had been reduced while the amount of dissipated power remains at 120 watts. This means that the power factor ratio after the correction is now closer to 1.0.

Practice Questions: Power Factor

Instructions: Select the best answer from the given choices.

1. Calculate the power factor of a circuit that has a real power of 960W and an apparent power of 1,000W.
    a. 1,960
    b. 40
    c. 1.04
    d. 0.96
2. Power factor is the ratio of real power to the apparent power in an AC electric circuit.
    a. True
    b. False
3. What is the power factor of a circuit that has a real power of 400 watts, a reactive power of 300 volt-amps-reactive, and apparent power of 500 watts?
    a. 0.5
    b. 0.6
    c. 0.7
    d. 0.8
4. The amount of useful power that is required to operate an electric blender is expressed in:
    a. Coulombs
    b. Volts
    c. Volt-Amps
    d. Watts
5. Determine the power factor of a 120-volt circuit that has fed an AC inductor motor that draws 10 amperes and has a real power of 720 watts.
    a. 0.2
    b. 0.4
    c. 0.6
    d. 0.8

Answer Key: Power Factor

1. d. 0.96

   To determine the answer, use this formula:

   $$Power\ Factor = \frac{Real\ Power}{Apparent\ Power}$$

   $$Power\ Factor = \frac{960\ watts}{1{,}000\ watts}$$

   $$Power\ Factor = 0.96$$

2. a. True

   Power factor is the ratio between the amount of power that is used (real power) and the amount of power that was being demanded (apparent power) by the system (circuit).

3. d. 0.8

   You don't need to consider the reactive power of the circuit to get the correct answer. Instead, use the standard formula:

   $$Power\ Factor = \frac{Real\ Power}{Apparent\ Power}$$

   $$Power\ Factor = \frac{400\ watts}{500\ watts}$$

   $$Power\ Factor = 0.8$$

4. d. watts

   Coulombs are typically used to measure electric charge. Volts is the standard unit of measure for voltage. Apparent power is represented in terms of volt-amps.

5. c. 0.8

   For this question, use the formula: $Power\ Factor = \frac{Real\ Power}{Apparent\ Power}$

   $$Power\ Factor = \frac{720\ watts}{120\ volts * 10\ amperes}$$

   $$Power\ Factor = \frac{720\ watts}{1{,}200\ volt-amps}$$

   $$Power\ Factor = 0.6$$

Chapter 4 – Codes

Whether it is your first time taking a licensing exam or you are already a licensed electrician, the National Electrical Code (NEC) book could be one of your best tools for success. As such, you need to learn how to find the information you are seeking in the book with minimal effort and maximum speed possible. This can be quite hard to achieve if you do not take the time to understand the outline and layout of the Code Book, as well as the effective approaches to look up the information you need at the time.

To boost your chances of passing the Journeyman Electrician Exam, this chapter goes over the layout of the NEC so that you will be more familiar with its contents. Tabbing important pages and highlighting critical details have also proven to enhance efficiency during the exam, so you will also learn about the right way to use page tabs and highlighters on your Code Book.

A section is also dedicated to the various methods that you can apply to improve the way you search for information in the book. The final part of this chapter will test how much you know the definitions of important electrical code terms, including international codes that all good electricians must know.

Electrical Codes

This refers to a set of regulations that must be observed when designing, installing, and inspecting electrical wiring systems in residential, commercial, and industrial settings. Through these codes, people can rest assured that various electrical hazards will not put anyone's safety at risk. Furthermore, the risk of damage or loss of assets due to electrical failure will be significantly reduced.

> "Electricity can be dangerous. My nephew tried to stick a penny into a plug. Whoever said a penny doesn't go far didn't see him shoot across that floor. I told him he was grounded."
>
> — Tim Allen

In the US, the prevailing electrical codes are compiled in the National Electrical Code (NEC). These codes are not set in stone, however. Every three years, the

NEC is revised based on technical discussions, inputs, and commentary from the experts, and public opinion of the codes.

Other than the NEC, you should also pay attention to the electrical codes, standards, and rules that are provided by the following:

- IEEE (Institute of Electrical and Electronics Engineers)
- NETA (International Electrical Testing Association)
- NFPA (National Fire Protection Association)
- OSHA (Occupational Safety and Health Administration)

Local ordinances, fire codes, and requirements for work or construction permits must also be taken note of when doing any electrical design, installation, or inspection.

International Codes

Other countries have also developed and adopted electrical codes to serve as guidance and reference for their electricians and anyone who wishes to design, install, or inspect electrical systems in their respective countries.

International codes also exist, where multiple countries observe and comply with the regulations specified in a single Code Book. For example, several countries under the European Union (EU) rely on the IEC 60364 for all electrical installations in buildings. These regulations are prepared and published by the International Electrotechnical Commission (IEC) so that the wiring standards of each EU member would be aligned with the IEC standards.

The IEC 60364 consists of multiple parts—some of which bear similarities with the NEC. For example, Part 4 of the IEC 60364 deals with protective measures for safety against different factors, such as electric shock, overcurrent, and voltage, among others. This is similar to Article 240 of the NEC, which contains information about overcurrent protection, and Article 242, which is about overvoltage protection.

The Eleven Components of the NEC

The NEC is organized and divided into eleven components that make its contents easier to understand and quicker to find.

A. Table of Contents
This resource page indicates the titles and corresponding page numbers of each chapter, article, and part. When faced with a situation that requires the guidance of the Code Book, smart electricians would first go to the table of contents and look for the portion of the NEC that is applicable at that moment.

B. Introduction to the National Electrical Code
Also known as "Article 90", this component contains information about the purpose of the Code Book, as well as its scope and limitations. You will also learn about the arrangement of the NEC in this introduction.

Other details included are as follow:
- Rules that are mandatory or permissive
- How the rules are to be enforced
- How the rules should be interpreted
- The importance of examining the safety of equipment
- Information about wiring plans
- Official formats for the units of measurement

C. Chapters
In total, the Code Book is made of nine chapters that cover different articles. These chapters may be grouped according to their respective scope, namely:
- General Requirements
  Chapters 1 to 4 belong to this group. The topics include wiring plans, means of protection, wiring methods, and materials, as well as equipment that are intended for general use.
- Specific Requirements
  In this group, you will find information about special occupancies, special equipment, and special conditions. The topics are covered across Chapters 5, 6, and 7.
- Communications Systems
  This group consists only of Chapter 8. However, it contains comprehensive information about different forms of

communications systems, such as telephone, data, satellite, cable TV, and broadband.
- Tables
Only Chapter 9 of the NEC falls under this group. Here you can find various tables about conduits, tubing, conductors, among others.

D. Articles
You can find an article for individual subjects in the NEC. There are about 140 articles in the Code Book—but do note that additional articles may be added with each new release. The most important articles that you should know and understand include but are not limited to:
- Article 100
This article contains the definitions for the important terms that the reader has to know to apply the Code requirements.
- Article 110
Refer to this article for an overview of the general requirements that must be considered when performing electrical installations.
- Articles 210, 240, and 250
These three articles focus on wiring design and protection. Everything you need to know about branch circuits, overcurrent protection, grounding, and bonding can be found there. You will find these articles useful when doing electrical calculations that will be covered in Chapter 5 of this book.
- Article 310

> **Helpful Tip!**
>
> Many electricians rely on Article 100 of the Code to resolve any confusion or miscommunication about electrical works. That's why you should not skip this article, thinking that your understanding of electrical concepts and theories would be enough to master the Code. Read through each definition so that you could effectively use the Code both during the licensing exam and in real-life applications.

Use this article to learn about the different types of electrical conductors.

- Articles 312 to 392

    This group of articles specifies the requirements for raceways, fittings, and boxes. You need to familiarize yourself with the contents of these articles for your electrical and load calculations.

- Article 404

    This article contains information about how to use switches as a means of controlling electrical circuits.

- Article 406

    Learn more about receptacles and convenience outlets, and the applicable Code requirements for each in this article.

- Article 410

    Refer to this article to learn how to properly install lighting fixtures.

- Article 430

    This covers the general information about electric motors.

- Articles 440 to 460

    These articles contain the Code requirements that are applicable to air conditioning units, heating equipment, transformers, and capacitors.

- Articles 500 to 503

    For more information about special occupancies that are at risk of exploding, read through the contents of these articles.

- Article 520

    Code requirements for theaters, auditoriums, and other similar locations can be found in this article.

- Article 620

    This article serves as a reference on how to install and operate elevators, escalators, and other similar electrical equipment.

- Article 700

    Information about emergency lighting systems can be found in this article.

- Articles 800 to 840

    Refer to these articles for the Code requirements that apply to communication systems.

E. Parts

To make large articles more readable and digestible, NEC subdivides such articles into parts. You won't be able to find information about parts in the section numbers so you should pay attention to them when you are tabbing or highlighting your Code Book.

Parts are marked using Roman numerals— like "I", "II", "III", "IV", etc. They also have titles that succinctly describe what the part is all about.

For example:
Article 399 – Future Products
I. General
II. Installation
III. Construction Specifications

Remember!

Some people in the industry refer to a Code Section as an "Article". Refrain from doing so yourself because that is improper. Remember: An NEC rule is called a section or code section. On the other hand, NEC articles are the individual subjects in the Code Book.

Others completely omit the words "section" or "code sections" when citing the rules, but only do so when it is not at the beginning of the sentence to avoid confusion.

F. Code Sections

Every rule in the NEC is referred to as a "Code Section". It may consist of sub-sections that are denoted by capital letters inside a pair of parentheses, such as (A), (B), (C), etc. If these lettered sub-sections are further broken down, the second-level sub-sections are marked with numbers in parentheses—for example, (1), (2), (3), etc. Meanwhile, the third-level sub-sections are denoted by small letters in parentheses like this: (a), (b), (c), etc.

Let's look at this example for Article 210 – Branch Circuits, Part I – General Provisions:

Section	210.5 Identification for Branch Circuits
First-Level Sub-Section	(A) Grounded Conductor (B) Equipment Grounding Conductor

Second-Level Sub-Section	(1) Branch Circuits Supplied for More Than One Nominal Voltage System (2) Branch Circuits Supplied from Direct-Current Systems
Third-Level Sub-Section	(a) Means of Identification (b) Posting of Identification Means

Quick Tip!

Use a short ruler or any similar straight-edged tool to make it easier to read through the contents of a table. The NEC has several tables that could take up large portions if not the whole page. Save time and reduce your chances of making an error with the aid of these tools.

G. Tables and Figures

The NEC organizes most of the code requirements in tables and figures. Pay careful attention to the title of each table and the caption of the figure. Through them, you will be able to understand what information the given table contains, as well as the contents' applications and limitations. Since a table or figure may be referenced in the text, each table or figure has its designated number, too.

Check if there are also notes within or below the table or figure. Read them as well because they are relevant to the code requirements.

For example:
In Section 500.8(C) - Marking, there is a table called "Table 500.8(C) – Classification of Maximum Surface Temperature.

H. Exceptions

These refer to permissions or requirements that offer an alternative approach for a specific requirement. In the NEC, there are two types of exceptions:
- Mandatory Exceptions
  You can tell if an exception is mandatory if uses the words "shall", "shall not" or "shall not be". If the exception used

"shall", then you must do it exactly as specified in the text. Similarly, the phrases "shall not" or "shall not be" indicate that you are not allowed to do it in the way described in that given exception.

- Permissive Exceptions
  This type uses the phrases "shall be permitted" or "shall be permissible" to state that it is acceptable but not required to do things in a certain way.

  The word "may" is also used, but only if an authority having jurisdiction can provide a discretionary judgment on the matter. You can also find this word being used in an Informational Note.

If several exceptions apply to the same rule, then the mandatory requirements are listed on top of the permissive exceptions.

I. Informational Notes
Aside from tables, Informational Notes may be found in other parts of the Code Book, too. They provide explanations that aim to clarify a rule or assist the reader in understanding the material.

However, these Informational Notes are not considered as part of the Code requirements. Therefore, they cannot be used to make interpretations or recommendations.

For example:
In Sub-Section (D) Volts Between Conductors, an Informational Note immediately follows this rule, suggesting to the reader to see Section 410.137 for information about auxiliary equipment limitations.

J. Annexes
Much like Information Notes, the Annexes are not part of the Code requirements. They serve as sources of further information only for the readers who want to learn more about topics that are relevant to the contents of the book.

Examples of content that you can find in the annexes are non-mandatory materials, examples of calculations, and other tables. Each annex is designated with a capital letter—such as "Informative

Annex A", "Informative Annex B", etc. Every annex also has a title indicating the type of information that can be found in it.

For example:
Informative Annex A – Product Safety Standards
Informative Annex H – Administration and Enforcement

K. Index
   This component is incredibly helpful for test-takers and practical situations, where you need to look up specific information in the Code Book.

How to Understand the Terms and Concepts of the Code Book

As mentioned earlier, the NEC exists for the guidance of people who know and understand terms, theories, practices, and procedures that are related to electrical works. Aside from electricians, other qualified individuals who should use the Code Book include electrical contractors, electrical designers, electrical engineers, and electrical inspectors. This means that the NEC is not for people who have no background or training at all.

Since you are already planning to take the Journeyman Electrician Exam, it is expected that you are at least familiar with the terms and concepts in the Code Book. This gives you a basic idea of how the NEC can be used to further your knowledge and acquire your license.

If you have gone through the previous section of this chapter, it is evident that the Code Book contains several important terms and their corresponding meanings and applications. Moreover, rules are specified for many of these terms so that the readers would understand the Code requirements for each.

To help you understand these terms and concepts, below are some key points that you should keep in mind:

> "The logic of a madman is a sane man's confusion."
>
> Joe R. Lansdale

- Several articles in the Code Book have definitions for terms that only apply to the content of the given article.
  For example, 760.2 contains definitions that are only applicable for the sections under Article 760 Fire Alarm Systems. Don't skip these unique definitions since your understanding of the Code requirements, exceptions, and tables within that article might not be comprehensive or accurate.

- Take note of simple words, such as "or" and "and".
  It's not enough that you only pay attention to the technical terms of the Code Book. Read carefully each sentence because even simple words can completely change the meaning of the definition or requirement. For instance, the word "and" can sometimes mean that the succeeding words are mandatory. On the other hand, the usage of the word "or" suggests that the reader can choose among the provided options.

- Use technical terms rather than slang.
  While you and your fellow electricians may understand a specific slang term, this does not mean that others in the field would also know what you mean. That is why it is important to learn the technical terms as stated in the Code Book. Through them, you can fully and effectively communicate trade-related matters with other professionals and even with your clients.

How to Tab the Code Book

The strategic placement of tabs throughout the Code Book will significantly improve your effectiveness and efficiency at looking up information about any electrical code that might be asked of you. It is also cost-effective because you can make it on your own using colored paper and adhesive tape. However, if you have some cash to spare, purchasing pre-made tabs will allow you to spend more time studying the Code Book rather than simply making it exam-ready.

Regardless if you are going to create or buy tabs, the best type of page tabs has the following qualities:

- Properly Labelled
  Each page tab must indicate the name of the code or table that it is signifying. Don't settle for just the code numbers because there is a

good chance that you would interchange things in your mind especially when you are in a rush or stressed out during the test.

Make sure that the font you use for the page tab is clear and large enough to read without straining your eyes. If the name of the code or table is too long for the size of the page tab, you can abbreviate or shorten the names—for example, the tab for Table 300.50 (Minimum Cover Requirements) may be labeled as "300.5 MIN. COVER REQTS."

- Color-Coded
Assigning colors to certain groups of page tabs is going to make the process a lot easier. Rather than read the labels one by one, you can filter your search by color first, and then proceed to narrow it down to the exact tab that you are looking for. If you buy pre-made tabs,

> **Quick Tip!**
>
> In general, sticky notes cannot be used as a substitute for page tabs during the licensing exam. If you decided to risk it, the testing center might not allow you to proceed with your exam. Create or purchase actual page tabs—preferably color-coded ones—for your Code Book.

physically adjacent codes or codes related to the topic are typically grouped and assigned with the same color.

For example, the page tabs for Code 700 (Emergency Systems), Code 702 (Optional Standby Systems), and Code 708 (Critical Operations Power Systems) may be red since these codes are not only physically adjacent to one another, but each of these codes deals with different types of electrical systems.

- Durable
Pre-made page tabs are usually made of laminated board paper or plastic. Such materials make the tabs withstand regular wear and tear that they may receive whenever you use the Code Book for the exam or work. If you plan to make your tabs, consider using the same or similar materials to ensure that you won't have to keep on replacing your page tabs now and then.

- Convenient
    The page tabs should not only improve the way you look up information from the Code Book. These tabs should also be easy to place along the page edges. Purchase page tabs that are pre-cut already so that all you have to do is stick them onto the Code Book.

You may opt to place tabs on every area covered by the NEC or only on certain pages that you frequently use as reference. Tabbing the Code Book is quick and easy no matter what your choice is. Normally, you would finish sticking on the page tabs within five to ten minutes only.

How to Highlight Key Information on the Code Book

The NEC is filled with vital information that you have to keep in mind to ensure safe electrical designs and installations. Unfortunately, this level of comprehensiveness makes the Code Book quite hard to read, especially for those who have just started studying the codes.

One effective way to hasten the process of searching for specific information is by breaking down each article and code into the following smaller chunks that are easier to find and remember. Below are some highlighting tips that could be of help to you:

- Assign different colors for each NEC component that you want to highlight.
    For example, use a yellow-colored highlighter for the parts of large articles. Pink highlighters may then be used for rules, while green highlighters can be used to distinguish mandatory exceptions from permissive exceptions.
    You may also highlight key details in the Table of Contents and Index so that you can find them quickly when needed.

- Practice restraint when highlighting the Code Book.
    As you study the articles and rules, you may get carried away and highlight everything—thinking that those would be relevant to you later on. Remember that by doing so, you are diminishing the effect of highlighting the Code Book because you won't be able to easily find the information you need in the sea of colored text.

- Underline or encircle keywords or key phrases.
  This works well when done to code requirements since it makes the important information pop out from the page, thus making them easier to locate later on. Use a red or blue pen to underline or encircle a certain portion of the Code Book. To make things more presentable and readable, use a 6-inch ruler for neater lines.

Methods of Looking Up Answers in the Code Book

The Journeyman Electrician Exam is an open-book activity. This means that you would be allowed to use your copy of the Code Book during the exam to search for the correct answer. The challenge, therefore, is not memorizing every rule word-for-word. Instead, how well you can find specific information in the NEC determines whether you would pass or fail the exam.

While you need to be at least familiar with the contents of the Code Book, another key goal during your exam preparation is to learn how to locate the required information in the Code Book as fast as possible. Therefore, speed and accuracy are the two keys to finishing within the time limit and with the highest score possible given your level of mastery of the electrical concepts and requirements that will be covered in the exam.

There are two primary ways on how you can look for specific information in the NEC: through the Table of Contents, and the Index. The best method for you depends on your level of experience in dealing with the Code Book. The most experienced Code users can refer to the correct rule without much effort. At most, they refer to the Table of Contents to look for the page number of a given definition, requirement, or table.

However, average and novice Code users should learn how to use the various tools that they can rely on to find the information they need.

Take Note!

For both methods described in this section, the common element is the keyword. Without identifying and highlighting the keyword, it would be hard for you to use any of the information look-up methods discussed in this book.

Method 1: Via the Table of Contents

To use this method, you need to have a good idea about which Article would apply to a term, requirement, or table that is being asked.

Let's say that the question is about the standard location for antenna discharge units. If you know your way around the NEC, you can immediately determine that the information you need is in Article 810 Radio and Television Equipment. That article is relatively large so the Code Book breaks it into four parts.

Given that the keywords for the information you are looking for are "antenna discharge units", you can immediately see in the Table of Contents that the answer you need is going to be in Part II Receiving Equipment – Antenna Systems.

When you turn the page to that part, you can then go through each section until you find the exact match to your words, which is Section 810.20 Antenna Discharge Units – Receiving Stations, sub-section (B) Location.

> **Quick Tip!**
>
> Since the NEC Index does not provide the page numbers where you can find the information you are looking for, feel free to write on the Index entry the page number and other helpful information that you would need to locate what you need as fast as possible. Use a pencil rather than a pen or a marker so that you can easily remove or modify your notes on the Index when needed.

Method 2: Via the Index

As discussed earlier, the Index is the NEC component that contains lists of the various subjects covered in the Code Book. They are listed in alphabetical order so you can easily find the keywords in the Index without having prior knowledge about the exact article or section it belongs.

Using the same example for Method 1, try looking up the keywords "antenna discharge units" in the Index. You will see among the terms listed under the letter "A" an exact match of the keywords. The Index states that it can be found in two sections: 810.20 and 810.57.

The question earlier is about the standard location for the antenna discharge units. Though 810.57 is about antenna discharge units as well, the information it contains focuses on the requirement for the conductors of units that are used as transmitting stations. Therefore, this section is not going to tell you the answer you are seeking. On the other hand, 810.20 is all about the location of antenna discharge units.

As you can see, the effectiveness of each method largely depends on how well you know the NEC. Since this is likely your first time taking the Journeyman Electrician Exam, it is highly recommended for you go through the lookup method via the Index to make the process faster and easier for you.

Practice Questions Set A: Codes

Instructions: Use the 2020 NEC to select the best answer from the given choices. Practice the lookup method via the Index to locate the information needed in the Code Book.

1. If an insulated ground conductor has a size of 6AWG, it may be identified through:
    a. a set of three continuous black and blue stripes
    b. a set of three continuous white and red stripes
    c. a continuous gray outer finish
    d. a continuous red outer finish
2. The use of Type AC cable is permitted:
    a. in cable trays
    b. in damp locations
    c. in locations exposed to corrosion
    d. none of the above
3. The ampacity for a 12-AWG fixture wire is:
    a. 8 amperes
    b. 17 amperes
    c. 23 amperes
    d. 28 amperes
4. Bends are not allowed in network broadband cables to prevent the cables from being damaged.
    a. True
    b. False
5. The maximum voltage limitations of control systems for permanent amusement attractions is _____ volts,

> **Something to Think About...**
>
> Which of these two methods do you think would serve you better while preparing for and taking the Journeyman Electrician Exam?

nominal, ac to the ground or _____ volts dc to ground.
  a. 150, 150
  b. 150, 300
  c. 300, 150
  d. 300, 300

6. In an area where the ambient temperature is 91 to 100°C, the correction factor of a conductor with a temperature rating of 200°C is:
  a. 0.67
  b. 0.79
  c. 0.83
  d. 0.85

7. The lead-in conductors for radio and television equipment must be made of which kind of material?
  a. Aluminum alloy
  b. Bronze
  c. Copper-clad steel
  d. All of the above

8. When necessary, flexible connections may be used for the wiring in Class II, Division 1 locations. In such cases, the following are permitted, except:
  a. Type LFMC with listed fittings
  b. Type LFNC with listed fittings
  c. Type ITC-HL cable with gastight sheath
  d. Type MC cable with interlocked armor

9. Resistors of over 1,000 volts, nominal, should not be installed near anything that may be considered a fire hazard. They should have a minimum clearance of _____ from any combustible materials.
  a. 12 mm
  b. 153 mm
  c. 305 mm
  d. 503 mm

10. The lighting load of a building that is designed and constructed to comply with the local authority's energy code is permitted to be calculated using the values indicated in the said energy code if certain conditions are met, such as:
  a. Application of a continuous load multiplier of 125%
  b. Feeder panel boards are properly labeled
  c. Appliances are not typically used at the same time
  d. The individual conductors are not smaller than 10 AWG copper

11. The indoor antenna of a wall-mounted television cannot run nearer than _____ to the conductors of other wiring systems in a house, except when the said conductors are placed in cable armor.
    a. 50 mm
    b. 100 mm
    c. 150 mm
    d. 200 mm
12. The markings of electrode-type boilers should indicate:
    a. the required electrical supply, including the frequency, number of wires, and phases
    b. a warning that reads, "All Power Supplies Shall Be Disconnected Before Servicing, Including Servicing the Pressure Vessel."
    c. the rating of the boiler in amperes, kilowatts, and volts
    d. all of the above
13. All supply circuits and interconnecting cables that have been identified for future use must have durable tags that bear which of the following information:
    a. Name of the manufacturer
    b. Frequency
    c. Date of installation
    d. Date of intended use
14. The proper installation of cellular concrete floor raceways requires for:
    a. the header to be installed in a diagonal line that is perpendicular to the cells
    b. the junction boxes to be sealed in a way that will prevent the entrance or concrete
    c. no markers since additional cells might be installed in the future
    d. Inserts that are made of nonmetallic materials
15. For power supply, the feeder assembly of a mobile home should consist of a listed mobile home power-supply cord rated _____ or feeder that has been installed permanently to the mobile home.
    a. 40 amperes
    b. 50 amperes
    c. 60 amperes
    d. 70 amperes
16. The spacing of 18 AWG aluminum conductor supports in vertical raceways shall not be greater than _____.
    a. 26 meters

b. 28 meters
   c. 30 meters
   d. 36 meters
17. Switches shall never disconnect the grounded conductor of a given circuit, except:
   a. when all conductors of the circuit are disconnected at the same time
   b. when the arrangement of the device prevents it from being disconnected unless all the ungrounded conductors of the circuit would be disconnected first
   c. either of the two exceptions given above
   d. there is no exception to this rule
18. In aircraft hangars, any equipment that is not recognized as suitable for _____ locations cannot be operated in locations where there is an ongoing maintenance operation that likely releases flammable vapors.
   a. Class I, Division 1
   b. Class I, Division 2
   c. Class II, Division 1
   d. Class II, Division II
19. What should the marking be for a non-power-limited fire alarm circuit cable?
   a. NPLF
   b. NPLFA
   c. NPLFP
   d. NPLFR
20. The minimum ampacity of continuous duty conductors that connects the secondary of a wound-rotor ac motor to its controller is _____ of the full-load secondary current of the motor.
   a. 75%
   b. 100%
   c. 125%
   d. 150%
21. The Code permits the usage of a flexible metal conduit with a metric designator larger than 103 (trade size 4).
   a. True
   b. False
22. Solar photovoltaic system equipment and disconnecting means cannot be installed in which of the following locations?
   a. Bedroom

b. Kitchen
c. Bathroom
d. Garage

23. The minimum size and type of equipment grounding conductors that are not an integral part of a cable assembly should be:
    a. 3 AWG aluminum
    b. 4 AWG copper
    c. 5 AWG aluminum
    d. 6 AWG copper

24. Which of the following type and sizes of grounding electrode conductor is not allowed for buildings without an intersystem bonding termination or grounding means?
    a. 8 AWG aluminum
    b. 10 AWG copper
    c. 17 AWG copper-clad steel
    d. 23 AWG bronze

25. If the nominal voltage to ground is from 151 to 600, the minimum clear distance for a working space that has exposed live parts on both sides is:
    a. 900 millimeters
    b. 1.0 meter
    c. 1.2 meters
    d. 1.5 meters

26. Decorative lightings for the holidays are permitted to remain installed for a maximum of _____ days.
    a. 60
    b. 70
    c. 80
    d. 90

27. What is the size range for the insulated conductors of an instrumentation tray cable?
    a. Sizes 14 AWG through 1 AWG
    b. Sizes 16 AWG through 8 AWG
    c. Sizes 18 AWG through 3 AWG
    d. Sizes 22 AWG through 12 AWG

28. The minimum strands for a 6-AWG PV wire are:
    a. 17
    b. 19
    c. 49

d. 130
29. The required clearance of a portable structure from any overhead conductors that operate at 600 volts or less is _____ unless a given conductor is supplying the portable structure.
    a. 4.5 meters
    b. 9 meters
    c. 13.5 meters
    d. 15 meters
30. The scope of the Code covers the installations of the:
    a. railways that are used for the generation, transmission, storage, or distribution of electric energy
    b. optical fibers for yards and parking lots
    c. outdoor communications equipment that is under the sole control of communications utilities
    d. electrical equipment in underground mines
31. The Code allows a coaxial cable to deliver power to equipment that is directly associated with the radio frequency distribution system if the voltage does not exceed:
    a. 50 volts
    b. 60 volts
    c. 70 volts
    d. 80 volts
32. All replaceable heating elements that are part of industrial process heating equipment must have a legible marking indicating the ratings in:
    a. amperes and watts
    b. amperes and temperature
    c. volts and watts
    d. volts and temperature
33. The size range that must be observed when using a High-Density Polyethylene (HDPE) Conduit has a maximum of _____ and a minimum of _____.
    a. metric designator 155 (trade size 6), metric designator 16 (trade size ½)
    b. metric designator 155 (trade size 6), metric designator 21 (trade size ¾)
    c. metric designator 103 (trade size 4), metric designator 16 (trade size ½)

d. metric designator 78 (trade size 3), metric designator 21 (trade size ¾)

34. The cable marking for a limited-use Class 3 cable is:
    a. CL3
    b. CL3P
    c. CL3R
    d. CL3X

35. Low-voltage lighting systems shall be supplied from a branch circuit with a maximum of _____.
    a. 5 amperes
    b. 10 amperes
    c. 20 amperes
    d. 40 amperes

36. Every patient bed under Category 2 (General Care) Spaces of healthcare facilities must be provided at least _____ receptacles.
    a. 4
    b. 8
    c. 12
    d. 16

37. The Code permits surge arresters to be located indoors but not outdoors because doing so will give unqualified persons access to the surge arresters.
    a. True
    b. False

38. The submersible pumps of a water fountain must operate at no more than _____ between conductors
    a. 100 volts
    b. 200 volts
    c. 300 volts
    d. 400 volts

39. Conductors of branch circuits that are used to supply power to multiple receptacles for portable loads with cord-and-plug connections should have an ampacity of _____.
    a. equal amount as the rating of the branch circuit
    b. not greater than the rating of the branch circuit
    c. not less than the rating of the branch circuit
    d. 150 amperes or more

40. What is the minimum size of a copper-clad steel conductor if the maximum open span length is more than 45 meters?

a. 10 AWG
b. 12 AWG
c. 14 AWG
d. 18 AWG

41. Which of the following types of the conduit is not permitted for Class III, Division 1 locations?
    a. Electrical metallic tubing
    b. High-density polyethylene conduit
    c. Intermediate metal conduit
    d. Rigid metal conduit

42. The Code expresses conductor sizes in:
    a. American Wire Gage (AWG)
    b. circular mils
    c. AWG or circular mils
    d. none of the above

43. The supports for an intermediate metal conduit can be placed at intervals that do not exceed:
    a. 3 meters
    b. 5 meters
    c. 8 meters
    d. 11 meters

44. The branch-circuit disconnecting means of a clock motor can serve as the controller since it is a stationary motor rated 1 horsepower and its construction prevents the motor from being damaged by overload.
    a. True
    b. False

45. The bonding conductor for communication systems must have a minimum size of:
    a. 12 AWG
    b. 14 AWG
    c. 16 AWG
    d. 18 AWG

46. Within enclosures, the conductors of intrinsically safe circuits must be prevented from having contact with the conductors of non intrinsically safe circuits by:
    a. separating the two types of conductors by at least 5 mm away from one another
    b. separating the two types of conductors with the use of metal sheathe or cladding

    c. using a grounded metal partition with a thickness of at least 0.91 mm
    d. using an approved insulating partition that can extend to the walls of the enclosure by 6.25 mm
47. A volatile flammable liquid has a:
    a. vapor pressure of below 276 kPa at a temperature of 38°C
    b. vapor pressure of below 38 kPa at a temperature of 276°C
    c. a flashpoint that is more than 38°C
    d. a flashpoint that is below 38°C
48. What is the demand factor that should be applied if there are 3 elevators on a single feeder?
    a. 1.00
    b. 0.95
    c. 0.90
    d. 0.85
49. Which type of non-power-limited fire alarm cable should be listed as having fire-resistance characteristics that prevent the spread of fire from floor to floor, and as being suitable for usage in a vertical run?
    a. Type NPLF
    b. Type NPLFA
    c. Type NPLFP
    d. Type NPLFR
50. A circuit breaker can serve as a switch if:
    a. it can be operated by hand and has a handle or a lever
    b. it is power-operated but can still be opened manually in case of a power failure
    c. if its number of poles is within the required amount
    d. all of the above
51. Aircraft batteries may be charged if they are installed in an aircraft that is partially inside a hangar, but not when the said aircraft is fully inside a hangar.
    a. True
    b. False
52. If used outside, the copper-clad bonding conductors of a radio or television cannot be installed within _____ of the earth.
    a. 400 mm
    b. 450 mm
    c. 500 mm
    d. 550 mm

53. Extra branch circuits are permitted if the capacity requirements of a given system are more than _____ at a supply voltage of _____ or less.
    a. 1,000 amperes, 1,000 volts
    b. 1,000 amperes, 2,000 volts
    c. 2,000 amperes, 1,000 volts
    d. 2,000 amperes, 2,000 volts
54. An electrified truck parking space supply equipment should be kept accessible through an entrance that is at least _____ wide and at least _____ high.
    a. 500 mm, 1.5 m
    b. 600 mm, 2.0 m
    c. 700 mm, 1.5 m
    d. 800 mm, 2.0 m
55. In theaters, the Code permits the usage of listed, hard usage cord if:
    a. there is adequate protection for the entire length of the cord from physical damage
    b. the branch circuit to which the cord is connected has an overcurrent protective device with a rating that is not more than 30 amperes
    c. the maximum length of the cord is 50 meters
    d. all of the above
56. To compensate for expansion and contraction due to heat, expansion fittings for PVC conduit must be provided. For example, the expected length of change of PVC conduit if the temperature change is $30^{\circ}C$ is:
    a. 0.30 mm/m
    b. 1.22 mm/m
    c. 1.83 mm/m
    d. 5.27 mm/m
57. The personnel door to be used as an entrance to or egress from a working space that has a piece of equipment rated 800A or more should be no less than _____ from the closest edge of the working space.
    a. 1.5 meters
    b. 4.2 meters
    c. 7.6 meters
    d. 9.5 meters
58. The proper switching sequence of series capacitors can be ensured by:
    a. using interlocks

b. isolating the overcurrent protection
c. setting a motor overload device
d. none of the above

59. Which of the following insulating media can be used for mounting the high-voltage parts of X-ray equipment within grounded enclosures?
    a. Air
    b. Rubber
    c. Plastic
    d. All of the above

60. For concealed knob-and-tube wiring, a minimum clearance of _____ must be maintained between each conductor.
    a. 25 mm
    b. 50 mm
    c. 75 mm
    d. 100 mm

61. Which of the following is not a permitted substitution for a conductive optical fiber riser cable?
    a. OFCG
    b. OFNP
    c. Both OFCG and OFNP
    d. Neither OFCG nor OFNP

62. All cables in agricultural buildings must be secured within _____ of each box, cabinet, or fitting.
    a. 100 mm
    b. 200 mm
    c. 300 mm
    d. 400 mm

63. The bonding conductor for communication systems shall be made of which of the following materials?
    a. alloy
    b. aluminum
    c. bronze
    d. copper

64. A branch-circuit overcurrent device shall not be located:
    a. in the vicinity of clothes closets or other materials that can be easily ignited
    b. inside the bathrooms of dwelling units or guest rooms
    c. over the steps of a stairway
    d. all of the above

65. In a television studio, the origin of the circuits of portable switchboards on stage should be from grounding-type polarized inlets of current and voltage that is _____ the fixed-load receptacle.
    a. greater than
    b. less than
    c. equal to
    d. half of
66. Which of the following is a required condition for range hoods to be installed and operated with a cord-and-plug-connected?
    a. The cord's length must not exceed 1.2 meters, but it should at least be 500mm long.
    b. The cord must have an equipment grounding conductor which can be terminated with the use of a grounding-type attachment plug.
    c. Receptacles must be in place to protect the cord from being physically damaged.
    d. An individual branch circuit supplies the receptacle for the range hood.
67. The conductors for installations that operate at less than 50 volts should not be smaller than _____ copper or its equivalent.
    a. 18 AWG
    b. 16 AWG
    c. 14 AWG
    d. 12 AWG
68. Type NMC cables are not permitted in motion picture studios and on elevators.
    a. True
    b. False
69. _____ conduit is not allowed in any pool area where corrosion of the material may occur.
    a. Aluminum
    b. Copper
    c. Nonmetallic
    d. All of the above
70. Which of the following types of fixed equipment must be enclosed in a bulk storage plant to prevent the escape of hot metal particles?
    a. attachment plugs
    b. flexible cords
    c. motors

d. pipelines
71. A charge controller is equipment that is used to control _____ voltage or _____ current, or both.
    a. ac, ac
    b. ac, dc
    c. dc, dc
    d. dc, ac
72. The receptacle rating for a circuit with a rating of 40 amperes is:
    a. not over 15 amperes
    b. between 15 and 20 amperes
    c. exactly 30 amperes
    d. either 40 or 50 amperes
73. A single hoist that is driven by two or more motors can be controlled by a single controller.
    a. True
    b. False
74. For usage aboveground, Reinforced Thermosetting Resin Conduit (RTRC) and fittings must be resistant to:
    a. impact and crushing
    b. effects of exposure to sunlight
    c. low temperature
    d. all of the above
75. The rating of a branch circuit supplying a neon tubing installation should not be more than:
    a. 10 amperes
    b. 20 amperes
    c. 30 amperes
    d. 40 amperes

Practice Questions Set B: Codes

Instructions: Use the 2020 NEC to select the best answer from the given choices. Practice the lookup method via the Index to locate the information needed in the Code Book.

1. Single-phase power sources in interactive systems must be connected to _____ power systems so that the unbalanced voltages at the point of interconnection will be limited to a maximum of _____.
    a. single-phase; 3 percent
    b. two-phase; 5 percent

    c. three-phase; 3 percent
    d. all-phase; 5 percent
2. _____ equipment has electrical components that can be moved by one person without requiring the aid of any mechanical aids.
    a. Light
    b. Minimal
    c. Portable
    d. Small
3. The Code considers a piece of electrical equipment with a potential difference of over _____, nominal, to be high voltage.
    a. 100 volts
    b. 300 volts
    c. 500 volts
    d. 1,000 volts
4. The spacing for 6-AWG copper-clad aluminum conductor supports in vertical raceways should not be greater than:
    a. 30 meters
    b. 41 meters
    c. 55 meters
    d. 60 meters
5. The source of energy for an electric organ must be supplied by a listed dc power supply with a maximum output of:
    a. 30 volts
    b. 45 volts
    c. 60 volts
    d. 75 volts
6. In healthcare facilities, the necessary unit equipment for backup illumination include:
    a. means of charging a battery
    b. provision for at least one lamp that is mounted on the equipment
    c. rechargeable battery
    d. all of the above
7. Multiple energy storage systems cannot be installed in the same building.
    a. True
    b. False

8. An overcurrent protective device that has a lower rating than the panelboard itself shall be placed within or at any point on the supply side of a panelboard, except:
    a. if protection is already provided by two main circuit breakers that have a combined rating greater than the panelboard's rating
    b. if the panelboard has a 3-pole circuit breaker
    c. if the panelboard contains over 42 overcurrent devices
    d. if the panelboard is used for an individual residency occupancy and it serves as a service equipment
9. A round box cannot be used if the conduit that requires the use of _____ must be connected to the side of the box.
    a. bushings
    b. fittings
    c. flexible cords
    d. insulated cables
10. The branch circuits for the HVAC equipment that is located within an elevator car has a maximum circuit voltage limit of:
    a. 500 volts
    b. 1,000 volts
    c. 1,000 volts
    d. 1,500 volts
11. What color should the braid be for an equipment grounding conductor?
    a. continuous blue color with one or more red stripes
    b. continuous green color with one or more yellow stripes
    c. continuous red color with one or more green stripes
    d. continuous yellow color with one or more blue stripes
12. When calculating branch-circuit, feeder, and service loads, rounding to the nearest whole ampere is only allowed if the fraction of an ampere is _____.
    a. greater than 0.5
    b. less than 0.5
    c. equal to 0.4
    d. equal to 0.9
13. In a one-family dwelling, the length of the grounding electrode conductor shall not exceed:
    a. 2 meters
    b. 4 meters

c. 6 meters
d. 8 meters
14. The watt density of an embedded snow-melting equipment should not exceed _____ of the heated area.
    a. 1,000 watts/m^2
    b. 1,100 watts/m^2
    c. 1,200 watts/m^2
    d. 1,300 watts/m^2
15. If the ceiling of a recreational vehicle is made of wood, all boxes and fittings must be _____ with the finished surface.
    a. embossed
    b. elevated
    c. flushed
    d. grounded
16. The maximum cord length for lighting with cord and plug connection in an office setting is:
    a. 0.9 meters
    b. 1.8 meters
    c. 2.7 meters
    d. 3.6 meters
17. Unless they are connected by receptacles or attachment plugs, luminaires should be installed in a way that will allow inspections to be conducted without having to disconnect the wiring.
    a. True
    b. False
18. The preferred measurement system of the Code is the:
    a. International Systems of Unit
    b. Linear Systems of Unit
    c. Imperial Systems of Unit
    d. None of the above
19. The markings of a Type MI cable must be a printed tag that is attached to the:
    a. carton
    b. coil
    c. reel
    d. any of the above
20. Stand-alone systems are permitted to supply three-phase:
    a. 1-wire systems
    b. 2-wire systems

c. 3-wire systems
d. all of the above

21. For feeders that supply transformers, the conductors shall not have an ampacity rating that is less than the total of the nameplate ratings of the transformers supplied.
    a. True
    b. False

22. The mandatory conditions for a combination thermostat to be considered as both controller and disconnecting means include:
    a. It is in a secluded location.
    b. The mark for the "off" position is provided.
    c. The mark for the "on" position is provided.
    d. It prevents the opening of any ungrounded conductors when manually turned off.

23. The voltage drop on any branch circuit of sensitive electronic equipment should not be more than _____, while the combined voltage drop of the branch-circuit conductors and feeder of sensitive electronic equipment should not be more than _____.
    a. 1.5%, 2.5%
    b. 1.5%, 5.0%
    c. 2.5%, 5.0%
    d. 2.5%, 6.5%

24. The construction specifications for conductors of Type P cables indicate that:
    a. the minimum conductor size is 12 AWG
    b. the material of the conductor is aluminum
    c. the conductor must employ flexible stranding
    d. all of the above

25. In which zone of the hazardous (classified) locations can you observe the continuous presence of ignitable fibers?
    a. Zone 20
    b. Zone 21
    c. Zone 22
    d. Zone 23

26. A circuit breaker that serves as a switch in 120-volt and _____ fluorescent lighting circuits shall be listed and marked SWD or HID.
    a. 240-volt
    b. 277-volt
    c. 323-volt

d. 450-volt
27. The automatic transfer switches of emergency systems should be:
    a. manually operated
    b. mechanically held
    c. reconditioned
    d. all of the above
28. The cord connector of a motor-compressor on a 15-ampere branch circuit must have a rating that cannot exceed _____ at 125 volts or _____ at 250 volts.
    a. 15 amperes, 20 amperes
    b. 20 amperes, 15 amperes
    c. 30 amperes, 40 amperes
    d. 40 amperes, 30 amperes
29. Which of the following is not a requirement for the rating plate provided for arc welders?
    a. Maximum ampacity
    b. Number of phases
    c. Rated primary current
    d. Basis of rating
30. The Code definition of a metal auxiliary gutter indicates that:
    a. It serves as protection for the electrical wires, cables, and busbars.
    b. It is used for locations that are wet or exposed to sunlight.
    c. Its housing has fixed covers that are secured with a lock.
    d. It is a sheet metal enclosure that is designed to be flame-retardant.
31. For storage batteries, a _____ cell must have a flame arrester to keep the cell from being destroyed if the gases within the cell are ignited due to a spark originating from the outside.
    a. dead
    b. live
    c. sealed
    d. vented
32. The minimum size of grounding conductors that are supplying small loads of only one branch circuit shall not be smaller than _____ hard-drawn copper or its equivalent.
    a. 4 AWG
    b. 8 AWG
    c. 12 AWG

d. 16 AWG
33. For locations under Divisions 1 and 2 of Class I, the melting point of the compound that provides a seal against gases and/or vapors should be:
   a. 93°C or higher
   b. 93°C or lower
   c. exactly 93°C
   d. exactly 100°C
34. The code letter marked on a nameplate of a motor with locked rotor kilovolt-ampere per horsepower of 13.00 is:
   a. A
   b. C
   c. M
   d. P
35. If a cable contains conductors operating more than _____, its marking should have a visible, permanently written, and easy to read warning notice that reads: "DANGER – HIGH VOLTAGE – KEEP AWAY"
   a. 300 volts
   b. 600 volts
   c. 900 volts
   d. 1,200 volts
36. This type of power-limited fire alarm cable is resistant to the spread of fire, and suitable for general-purpose fire alarm use with some exceptions such as, but not limited to, ducts and plenums.
   a. Type FPL
   b. Type FPLA
   c. Type FPLP
   d. Type FPLR
37. The minimum dimensions of clear working space for a motion picture projector should be _____ wide on every side and at the rear.
   a. 500 mm
   b. 750 mm
   c. 1,000 mm
   d. 1,250 mm
38. The ampacity of a 4,000-KCMIL Type IGS Cable is:
   a. 476 amperes
   b. 491 amperes
   c. 505 amperes
   d. 519 amperes

39. What is the medium that allows the transportation of ions between a cell's positive and negative electrodes?
    a. battery
    b. container
    c. electrolyte
    d. nominal voltage
40. Other than industrial establishments, the usage of open wiring on insulators is also permitted for:
    a. agricultural establishments
    b. commercial establishments
    c. residential properties
    d. none of the above
41. Which of the following is a permitted substitution for a communications riser cable?
    a. Communications general-purpose cable
    b. Communications plenum cable
    c. Under-carpet communications wire and cable
    d. None of the above
42. The service disconnecting means for a one-family dwelling must have a rating of _____.
    a. not greater than 100 amperes, 6-wire
    b. not greater than 100 amperes, 3-wire
    c. not less than 100 amperes, 6-wire
    d. not less than 100 amperes, 3-wire
43. How many overload units are needed for a 1-phase ac motor that has a 3-phase supply system?
    a. 0
    b. 1
    c. 2
    d. 3
44. For medium voltage conductors, the conductor shall be made of _____, unless otherwise specified.
    a. aluminum
    b. copper
    c. aluminum-clad copper
    d. any of the above
45. A storable swimming pool can have a flexible cord that has a maximum length of:
    a. 600 mm

- b. 700 mm
- c. 800 mm
- d. 900 mm

46. The doorway of a transformer vault should not have:
    - a. a fire rating of 3 hours or higher
    - b. a door sill that is below 100 mm
    - c. a lock and key
    - d. all of the above

47. The overall length of a power-supply cord for a mobile home must have a minimum length of _____ and a maximum length of _____. This should be measured from the end of the cord up to the face of the attachment plug cap.
    - a. 6.4 meters, 11 meters
    - b. 6.4 meters, 15 meters
    - c. 7.1 meters, 11 meters
    - d. 7.1 meters, 15 meters

48. A set of fuses that can be operated as a disconnecting switch is permitted to be the isolating switch.
    - a. True
    - b. False

49. The minimum radius for fixed bends of an Electric Nonmetallic Tubing (ENT) with a metric designator of 16 (trade size ½) is:
    - a. 88.9 mm
    - b. 101.6 mm
    - c. 127.0 mm
    - d. 317.5 mm

50. Which type of electromechanical connector is used for the interconnection busbars so that they hang from a certain ceiling grid rail to another nearby grid rail?
    - a. Load Connector
    - b. Pendant Connector
    - c. Power Feed Connector
    - d. Rail to Rail Connector

51. The minimum distance of flange openings of flameproof enclosure "d" from obstructions is:
    - a. 40 mm for Gas Group IIA
    - b. 40 mm for Gas Group IIB
    - c. 40 mm for Gas Group IIC
    - d. 40 mm for Gas Group IID

52. The construction specifications of a flexible cord state that:
    a. It must have aluminum flexible stranding
    b. Before being labeled and shipped, it must undergo examination and testing at the factory
    c. The conductor's nominal thickness of insulation should be fixed at 0.76 mm
    d. All of the above
53. Industrial heating appliances must have overcurrent protection of not greater than _____.
    a. 50 amperes
    b. 100 amperes
    c. 150 amperes
    d. 200 amperes
54. The marking of a busway must include the name of the manufacturer or the trademark, as well as the voltage and current rating according to its design.
    a. True
    b. False
55. A generator with a rating of over _____ must have a provision for a remote emergency shutdown switch that is located outside its enclosure or the equipment room.
    a. 1 kilowatt
    b. 5 kilowatts
    c. 10 kilowatts
    d. 15 kilowatts
56. Metal wireways are not permitted to be used in:
    a. any hazardous (classified) locations
    b. any wet locations
    c. any severely corrosive environments
    d. any concealed spaces
57. The nameplate of a load-interrupter switch must:
    a. be permanent and legible
    b. indicate the continuous current rating
    c. include the maximum voltage rating
    d. all of the above
58. The applicable feeder demand factor for the first 50,000 volt-amp portion of a stage set lighting load is:
    a. 50%
    b. 60%

c. 75%
d. 100%

59. Extending a metal multioutlet assembly through dry partitions is allowed if:
    a. there is no outlet located within the same dry partitions
    b. some portions will be left exposed
    c. it will also serve as a pull box
    d. none of the above

60. Busbars and conductors on a switchboard must be arranged in a way that prevents overheating due to capacitive effects.
    a. True
    b. False

61. Which color code should be used to identify intrinsically safe conductors, assuming that there are no other conductors of the same color within the same system?
    a. Light gray
    b. Light pink
    c. Light blue
    d. Light green

62. The nameplate of a transformer should indicate:
    a. frequency
    b. the primary and secondary voltage
    c. rated kVA
    d. all of the above

63. The depth of a box that encloses a device supplied by a conductor with a size of 14 AWG or smaller should not be less than:
    a. 23.8 mm
    b. 25.0 mm
    c. 30.2 mm
    d. 52.4 mm

64. A discharge circuit can be manually switched or connected to the terminals of a capacitor bank.
    a. True
    b. False

65. The contact conductors for electric cranes in locations under Class III, Divisions 1 and 2 must:
    a. have a power supply that is isolated from other systems
    b. be in a safe and secured area that is only accessible to authorized personnel

c. be protected from making accidental contact with a foreign object
d. all of the above

66. If the loads to be supplied to a phase converter is variable, then the ampacity of the conductor must not be _____ of the phase converter single-phase input full-load amperes.
    a. greater than 125%
    b. less than 125%
    c. exactly 125%
    d. none of the above

67. The temperature class T3C has a maximum surface temperature of:
    a. 160°C
    b. 230°C
    c. 320°C
    d. 450°C

68. Flammable gas belongs to which Class I group classifications of hazardous (classified) locations:
    a. Group A
    b. Group B
    c. Group C
    d. Group D

69. The size of the supply conductor for modular data centers must have an ampacity that does not exceed _____ of the full-load current rating.
    a. 75%
    b. 100%
    c. 125%
    d. 150%

70. In the case that non-heating leads for embedded equipment enter a metal raceway, insulated bushings must be used in:
    a. asphalt
    b. concrete
    c. masonry
    d. all of the above

71. Other than an approved automatic fire protection system, in what kind of spaces can the feeder-circuit equipment of emergency systems be located?
    a. A space with a 1-hour fire-resistance rating
    b. A space with a 2-hour fire-resistance rating
    c. A space with a 3-hour fire-resistance rating

d. None of the above
72. The Code requires the cell line working zone for electrolytic cells to extend through roofs, walls, and floors.
    a. True
    b. False
73. The permitted types of luminaires in clothes closets are:
    a. incandescent luminaires with partially enclosed lamps
    b. lampholders
    c. pendant luminaires
    d. recessed fluorescent luminaires
74. For the floodplain-protection of critical operations power systems (COPS), the feeders that are installed below the 100-year floodplain level must:
    a. have insulated circuit conductors that are listed for use in wet locations
    b. have applied a wiring method that is permitted for damp locations
    c. have overcurrent protection devices that are located above the 100-year floodplain level
    d. all of the above
75. All energized equipment parts of fire pumps must be located at least _____ above the floor level.
    a. 100 mm
    b. 200 mm
    c. 300 mm
    d. 400 mm

Answer Key Set A: Codes

Note: All references provided below can be found in the 2020 NEC.

1. c. a continuous gray outer finish
   Reference: 200.6(A)(2)

2. a. in cable trays
   Reference: 320.10

3. c. 23 amperes
   Reference: Table 402.5

4. b. False
   Reference: 830.160

5. b. 150, 300
   Reference: 522.5

6. b. 0.79
   Reference: Table 310.15(B)(2)

7. d. All of the above
   Reference: 810.11

8. c. Type ITC-HL cable with gastight sheath
   Reference: 502.10(A)(2)

9. c. 305 mm
   Reference: 470.18(D)

10. a. Application of a continuous load multiplier of 125%
    Reference: 220.12(B)

11. a. 50 mm
    Reference: 810.18(B)

12. d. all of the above
    Reference: 425.86

13. d. Date of intended use
    Reference: 645.5(H)(2)

14. b. the junction boxes to be sealed in a way that will prevent the entrance or concrete
    Reference: 372.18(C)

15. b. 50 amperes
    Reference: 550.10(A)

16. c. 30 meters
    Reference: Table 300.19(A)

17. c. either of the two exceptions given above
    Reference: 404.2(B)

18. b. Class I, Division 2
    Reference: 513.10(D)(3)

19. a. NPLF
    Reference: Table 760.176(G)

20. c. 125%
    Reference: 430.23(A)

21. b. False
    Reference: 348.20(B)

22. c. Bathroom
    Reference: 690.4(E)

23. d. 6 AWG copper
    Reference: 250.190(C)(1)

24. d. 23 AWG bronze
    Reference: 810.21(H)

25. c. 1.2 meters
    Reference: Table 110.26(A)(1)

26. d. 90
    Reference: 590.3(B)

27. d. Sizes 22 AWG through 12 AWG
    Reference: 727.6

28. c. 49
    Reference: Table 690.31(C)(4)

29. a. 4.5 meters
    Reference: 525.5(B)(1)

30. b. optical fibers for yards and parking lots
    Reference: 90.2(A)(2)

31. b. 60 volts
    Reference: 820.15

32. c. volts and watts
    Reference: 425.29

33. a. metric designator 155 (trade size 6), metric designator 16 (trade size ½)
    Reference: 353.20(A) and 353.20(B)

34. d. CL3X
    Reference: Table 725.179(J)

35. c. 20 amperes
    Reference: 411.7

36. b. 8
    Reference: 517.18(B)(1)

37. b. False
    Reference: 242.46

38. c. 300 volts
    Reference: 680.51(B)

39. c. not less than the rating of the branch circuit
    Reference: 210.19(A)(2)

40. b. 12 AWG
    Reference: Table 810.52

41. b. High-density polyethylene conduit
    Reference: 503.10(A)(1)

42. c. AWG or circular mils

Reference: 110.6

43. a. 3 meters
    Reference: 342.30(B)

44. b. False
    Reference: 430.81(A)

45. b. 14 AWG
    Reference: 800.100(3)

46. c. using a grounded metal partition with a thickness of at least 0.91 mm
    Reference: 504.30(A)(2)

47. d. a flashpoint that is below 38°C
    Reference: 100 Volatile Flammable Liquid

48. c. 0.90
    Reference: Table 620.14

49. d. Type NPLFR
    Reference: 760.176(D)

50. d. all of the above
    Reference: 404.11

51. b. False
    Reference: 513.10(A)(2)

52. b. 450 mm
    Reference: 810.21(A)

53. c. 2,000 amperes, 1,000 volts
    Reference: 225.30 (D)

54. b. 600 mm, 2.0 m
    Reference: 626.22(C)

55. a. there is adequate protection for the entire length of the cord from physical damage
    Reference: 520.68(A)(2)

56. c. 1.83 mm/m
    Reference: Table 352.44(A)

57. c. 7.6 meters
    Reference: 110.26(C)(3)

58. a. using interlocks
    Reference: 460.24(C)

59. a. Air
    Reference: 660.47(A)

60. c. 75 mm
    Reference: 394.19(A)

61. a. OFCG
    Reference: Table 770.154(b)

62. b. 200 mm
    Reference: 547.5(B)

63. d. copper
    Reference: 800.100(A)(2)

64. d. all of the above
    Reference: 240.24(E)

65. c. equal to
    Reference: 520.50(B)

66. a. The cord's length must not exceed 1.2 meters, but it should at least be 500mm long.
    Reference: 422.16(B)(4)

67. d. 12 AWG

Reference: 720.4

68. a. True
    Reference: 334.12(A)

69. a. Aluminum
    Reference: 680.25(B)

70. c. motors
    Reference: 515.7(B)

71. c. dc, dc
    Reference: 100 Charge Controller

72. d. either 40 or 50 amperes
    Reference: Table 210.21 (B)(3)

73. a. True
    Reference: 610.51(A)

74. d. all of the above
    Reference: 355.100

75. c. 30 amperes
    Reference: 600.5(C)(1)

Answer Key Set B: Codes
Note: All references provided below can be found in the 2020 NEC.

1. c. three-phase; 3 percent
   Reference: 705.45(A)

2. c. Portable
   Reference: 100 Portable Equipment

3. d. 1,000 volts
   Reference: 490.2

4. d. 60 meters

Reference: Table 300.19(A)

5. a. 30 volts
   Reference: 650.4

6. d. all of the above
   Reference: 517.2

7. b. False
   Reference: 706.6

8. d. if the panelboard is used for an individual residency occupancy and it serves as a service equipment
   Reference: 408.36

9. a. bushings
   Reference: 314.2

10. b. 1,000 volts
    Reference: 620.3(C)

11. b. continuous green color with one or more yellow stripes
    Reference: 400.23(B)

12. a. greater than 0.5
    Reference: 220.5(B)

13. c. 6 meters
    Reference: 770.100(A)(4)

14. d. 1,300 watts/m2
    Reference: 426.20(A)

15. c. flushed
    Reference: 551.47(D)

16. c. 2.7 meters
    References: 605.6(B)

17. a. True
    Reference: 410.8

18. a. International Systems of Unit
    Reference: 90.9(A)

19. d. any of the above
    Reference: 310.8(B)(3)

20. c. 3-wire systems
    Reference: 710.15(D)

21. a. True
    Reference: 215.2(B)(1)

22. b. The mark for the "off" position is provided.
    Reference: 424.20(A)

23. a. 1.5%, 2.5%
    Reference: 647.4(D)

24. c. the conductor must employ flexible stranding
    Reference: 337.104

25. c. Zone 22
    Reference: 506.6(B)(1)

26. b. 277-volt
    Reference: 240.83(D)

27. b. mechanically held
    Reference: 700.5(C)

28. b. 20 amperes, 15 amperes
    Reference: 440.55(B)

29. a. Maximum ampacity
    Reference: 630.14

30. a. It serves as protection for the electrical wires, cables, and busbars.
    Reference: 366.2

31. d. vented
    Reference: 480.11(A)

32. c. 12 AWG
    Reference: 230.23(B)

33. a. 93°C or higher
    Reference: 501.15(C)(2)

34. d. P
    Reference: Table 430.7(B)

35. b. 600 volts
    Reference: 392.18(H)

36. a. Type FPL
    Reference: 760.179(F)

37. b. 750 mm
    Reference: 540.12

38. a. 476 amperes
    Reference: Table 326.80

39. c. electrolyte
    Reference: 480.2

40. a. agricultural establishments
    Reference: 398.10

41. b. Communications plenum cable
    Reference: Table 805.179

42. d. not less than 100 amperes, 3-wire
    Reference: 230.79(C)

43. b. 1
    Reference: Table 430.37
44. d. any of the above
    Reference: 311.12(B)

45. d. 900 mm
    Reference: 680.8(A)

46. b. a door sill that is below 100 mm
    Reference: 450.43(B)

47. a. 6.4 meters, 11 meters
    Reference: 550.10(D)

48. a. True
    Reference: 230.204(B)

49. b. 101.6 mm
    Reference: Table 360.24(8)

50. d. Rail to Rail Connector
    Reference: 393.2

51. c. 40 mm for Gas Group IIC
    Reference: Table 505.7(D)

52. b. Before being labeled and shipped, it must undergo examination and testing at the factory
    Reference: 400.21(A)

53. a. 50 amperes
    Reference: 422.11 (C)

54. a. True
    Reference: 368.120

55. d. 15 kilowatts
    Reference: 445.18(C)

56. c. any severely corrosive environments
    Reference: 376.12

57. d. all of the above
    Reference: 490.21(E)(3)

58. d. 100%
    Reference: Table 530.19(A)

59. a. there is no outlet located within the same dry partitions
    Reference: 380.76

60. b. False
    Reference: 408.3(B)

61. c. Light blue
    Reference: 504.80(C)

62. d. all of the above
    Reference: 450.11(A)

63. a. 23.8 mm
    Reference: 314.24(B)(5)

64. b. False
    Reference: 460.6(B)

65. d. all of the above
    Reference: 503.155(A) and 503.155(B)

66. b. less than 125%
    Reference: 455.6(A)(1)

67. a. 160°C
    Reference: Table 500.8(C)

68. b. Group B
    Reference: 500.6(A)(2)

69. c. 125%
   Reference: 646.6(A)

70. d. all of the above
   Reference: 426.22(C)

71. b. a space with a 2-hour fire-resistance rating
   Reference: 700.10(D)(3)

72. b. False
   Reference: 668.10(B)

73. d. recessed fluorescent luminaires
   Reference: 410.16(A)

74. a. have insulated circuit conductors that are listed for use in wet locations
   Reference: 708.10(C)(3)

75. c. 300 mm
   Reference: 695.12(D)

Chapter 5 – Electrical Calculations & Load Calculations

As part of your preparation for the Journeyman Electrician Exam, you have to practice doing electrical calculations and load calculations based on the electrical laws, theories, and Code requirements. Possessing this ability would also serve you well while doing actual field work since many aspects of an electrician's work depend on how well you know the equations and tables.

Before jumping into the different types of calculations that would likely be covered in the licensing exam, let's go over the basics of the so-called "electrician's math" first.

- Different Forms of Numbers
  As you go along this chapter, you will notice that numbers in electrical calculations take various forms: whole numbers (0, 1, 2, 3, etc.), decimals (0.23, 1.85, 10.05, etc.), fractions (½, ¼, 3 ½, 5 ¼, etc.), and percentages (13%, 28%, 95%, etc.)

  You need to know how to convert one form to another to complete some electrical calculations. For example, the fraction ½ is equivalent to 50% in percentage form.

- Imperial System to Metric System
  As explained in the previous chapter, the NEC has officially adapted the metric system. However, since the application of its rules, requirements, and guidelines are based on the US, it is not uncommon for you to encounter values that are expressed using imperial units of measurement, such as inches and feet.

  To make calculations easier, memorize some of the frequently performed conversions between or within the two systems. For example, 1 inch is equal to 2.54 centimeters or 25.4 millimeters. On the other hand, 1 kilometer is equivalent to 0.613 miles or 1,000 meters.

- Rounding Off Numbers
  The Code does not require a specific number of significant figures for decimals. However, in general, electrical calculations use up to 3 digits—for example, 8.297 or 6.22.

If the last digit of a decimal number is below 5, then the number can be rounded down. On the other hand, if the last digit is 5 or higher, then it can be rounded up.
- 8.1693 -> 8.169 (rounded down because "3" is below "5")
- 11.278 -> 11.28 (rounded up because "8" is greater than "5")
- 10.5 -> 11 (rounded up because the last digit is "5")

- Basic Algebra
Having a basic knowledge of algebra would serve you well, especially when you have to derive the formula for what is being asked in the given scenario from another existing formula. If you had gone through Chapters 2 and 3 of this book, then you would have already seen examples of how this goes.

Remember to brush up on your algebra skills so that you would have a better chance of arriving at the correct answer for the different types of calculations that will be covered by the exam.

- Substitution as a Means of Checking
The great thing about mathematical calculations is that you can check the accuracy of your answer through substitution. To do this, take the answer you have calculated, and input that into the formula that you have used. Then, omit another element of the equation—one that has a given value in the question—and then check if you can arrive at that value using your calculated answer that has been inputted in the formula you have used earlier.

To better illustrate this, let's say that the question is asking about the voltage of a circuit with a current flow of 5 amperes and a resistance value of 6 ohms. Using the standard Ohm's Law formula for voltage, your answer is 30 volts. As a way of checking if your answer is correct or not, you decided to substitute the value of "E" in the formula, and look for the resistance of the circuit instead.
- Original Calculation

$$E = I * R$$

Quick Tip!
In case you are not sure up how many significant figures should be in your calculations, just follow the number of significant figures used in the question or scenario.

$E = 5\ amperes * 6\ ohms$

$E = 30\ ohms$

- Substitution

$$R = \frac{E}{I}$$

$$R = \frac{30\ volts}{5\ amperes}$$

$R = 6\ ohms$

As you can see, the resistance of 6 ohms has been obtained using the voltage you have calculated originally. This means that the voltage for the given circuit is 30 volts.

Every test taker has a different level of mathematical skills and understanding. As such, you may find this chapter as either a stroll on the beach or a hike up a mountain. Regardless, you need to spend time learning the different types of electrical calculations and load calculations that are explained in this chapter. By doing so, you would find the licensing exam less daunting since you're confident that you know your way around the numbers and formulas involved in your chosen trade.

Box Fill Calculations

Electricians need to know how to do box fill calculations before proceeding with any installations or while conducting an inspection. By doing so, they will determine if a given electrical box is overfilled with not just wires, but also conductors, fittings, and other electrical devices.

While you may see signs of overcrowding through a glance of an electrical box, you cannot be completely certain that it is over the standards until you have performed a box fill calculation.

According to the Code, every electrical box can only fit a certain volume of conductors, devices, and parts to remain safe

> **Take Note!**
>
> A box fill calculation is relatively easy to do, but it would be helpful to have a calculator on standby while doing this part of the licensing exam. Remember, you only have a limited time to finish answering all the questions, and you would likely need to refer to the relevant tables to confirm if the calculated volume is within the standards of the Code.

for its users. You can refer to Table 314.16(A) for the volume of these components. If it can't be found there, check the markings of the given component to see if its volume is indicated and expressed in cubic inches.

The trade size of the common metallic electrical boxes with their corresponding volumes can also be found in the same table. In the same table, you will also find the number of conductors that are allowed for each type of box.

Take note that these standards are under the assumption that the conductors are of the same sizes. If this is the case for the electrical box in question, you can use Table 314.16(A) to find out how many conductors are permitted for that box or to determine the appropriate size of the box for a certain number of conductors.

If the conductors used are not uniform in size, Table 314.16(B) specifies the requirements for different sizes of conductor, ranging from 6 AWG up to 18 AWG.

Examples of Box Fill Calculations

First, let's cover this example of a 4-inch electrical box that contains six THHN conductors and 3 THW conductors—all of which are sized 12 AWG. Given the expected volume, what should be the minimum depth of the said electrical box?

First, get the total count of the conductors of the same sizes. In box fill calculations, the type of insulation does not matter so you can get the sum of the THHN and THW conductors since they are both 12 AWG.

$$6\ THHN\ conductors + 3\ THW\ conductors = 9\ conductors\ (12\ AWG)$$

Next, check the standards stated in Table 314.16(A) for the correct answer. According to the table, the minimum depth of the box should be 4 x 1 ½ square inches.

Now, what if the conductors to be placed in the 4 x ½ square-inch electrical box are sized 14 AWG instead?

You can use Table 314.16(A) again to find out the maximum count of 14-AWG conductors that are permitted in the box. Based on the table, the upper limit of the box is seven 14-AWG conductors.

How about the computation for boxes with differently sized conductors?

For this scenario, let's say that a square metallic electrical box has the following trade size dimensions: 4 inches x $2\frac{1}{8}$ inches.

If you would at Table 314.6(A), the maximum capacity of this box is 30.3 in³ (497 cm³).

This box contains the following components:

- #12 NM (Nonmetallic) cable
    - Quantity: 2 pieces
- # 14 NM cable
    - Quantity: 1 piece
- Internal cable clamp
    - Quantity: 2 pieces
- Device yoke
    - Quantity: 1 piece
- Luminaire mounting stud
    - Quantity: 1 piece
- Grounding conductor
    - Quantity: 3 pieces, one for every NM cable

All of the given conductors are terminated or spliced within the box. Based on this information, is the electrical box in question within standard?

To find out the answer, let's calculate first the volume allowance for each component. Refer to Table 314.16(B) to get information about the required volume allowances per conductor.

- #12 NM (Nonmetallic) cable
    - No. of Conductors: 4

- Volume Allowance: 9 in³ (147.6 cm³)
- Basis:

$$4 \times 2.25 \ in^3 = 9 \ in^3$$

or

$$4 \times 36.9 \ cm^3 = 147.6 \ cm^3$$

- #14 NM cable
  - No. of Conductors: 2
  - Volume Allowance: 4 in³ (65.6 cm³)
  - Basis:

$$2 \times 2.00 \ in^3 = 4 \ in^3$$

or

$$2 \times 32.8 \ cm^3 = 65.6 \ cm^3$$

- Cable clamps
  - Volume Allowance: Single; 2.25 in³ (36.9 cm³)
  - Basis: Size of the largest conductor
- One device yoke
  - Volume Allowance: Double; 4.5 in³ (73.8 cm³)
  - Basis: Size of the largest conductor that is connected to the device

$$2 \times 2.25 \ in^3 = 4.5 \ in^3$$

or

$$2 \times 36.9 \ cm^3 = 73.8 \ cm^3$$

- One luminaire mounting stud
  - Volume Allowance: 2.25 in³ (36.9 cm³)
  - Basis: Single volume allowance based on the size of the largest conductor
- Grounding conductors
  - Volume Allowance: 2.25 in³ (36.9 cm³)
  - Basis: Single volume allowance based on the size of the largest conductor

The next step is to get the sum of these volume allowances:

$$9\ in^3 + 4\ in^3 + 2.25\ in^3 + 4.5\ in^3 + 2.25\ in^3 + 2.25\ in^3 = 24.25\ in^3$$

or

$$147.6\ cm^3 + 65.6\ cm^3 + 36.9\ cm^3 + 73.8\ cm^3 + 36.9\ cm^3 + 36.9\ cm^3 = 397.7\ cm^3$$

As mentioned earlier, this given box has a maximum capacity of is 30.3 in³ (497 cm³). Since the total volume allowance is just 24.25 in³ (397.7 cm³), this installation complies with the Code.

But what if the size of the electric box is not included in Table 314.16(A)? How would you be able to tell if it is a safe installation or not?

Again, it is just a matter of calculating the volume allowances of every component of the box at hand. Then, check which of the listed boxes in the table would be able to safely contain everything in the box.

If the size of the box in question is smaller than the one stated in the table, then it is not compliant. Conversely, a box that is larger than the one in the table is considered a safe installation.

Through this method, you will also be able to find out the appropriate size of the electrical box based on the components that it is going to contain. If the box fill is more than the box volume, you must either lessen the conductors that will be installed or replace the box with a larger one.

To sum things up:

- If you are sizing an electrical box that contains same-sized conductors, just add all these conductors and refer to Table 314.16(A) for the standard-compliant box size.

> "If the size of the box in question is smaller than the one stated in the table, then it is not compliant. Conversely, a box that is larger than the one in the table is considered a safe installation."

- If conductors of different sizes will fill an electrical box, go to Table 314.16(B) instead to find out information about each conductor. Get the sum of their volume before checking Table 314.16(A) for the appropriate size of the given box.

Practice Questions: Box Fill Calculations

Instructions: Select the best answer from the given choices.

1. A square box with a size of 4 inches by 1 ½ inch is adequate for nine 18-AWG conductors since it does not contain any clamps, support fittings, devices, equipment, or equipment grounding conductors.
    a. True
    b. False

2. What is the maximum number of 12-AWG conductors that can be installed in an electrical box that has a marking of 60 in^3 as its volume?
    a. 24
    b. 25
    c. 26
    d. 27

3. Determine the minimum volume of a 2-gang nonmetallic box that used Type NM cable as the wiring method, and has internal clamps for the security of the cables. The outlet circuit has two 12-AWG cables, while for the lighting circuit, the box has two 14-AWG cables and three 14-AWG cables. The box is used for a 3-way switch and a duplex receptacle outlet.
    a. 8 cubic inches
    b. 16 cubic inches
    c. 24 cubic inches
    d. 32 cubic inches

4. What are the required minimum depth for a 4-inch electric box that has cable clamps, one 12/2 w/G Type NM cable that terminates on a receptacle, and one 14/3 w/G Type NM cable that has a 3-way switch as its termination?
    a. 4 x ¼ square inches
    b. 4 x ½ square inches
    c. 4 x 2 1/8 square inches
    d. None of the above

5. How many 14-AWG conductors can be added to a 4 x 2 1/8 square electric box if it has two receptacles, five 12-AWG conductors, one 12-AWG equipment grounding conductor, and a plaster ring of 3.60 cubic inches?
    a. 4 conductors

		b. 5 conductors
		c. 6 conductors
		d. 7 conductors

Answer Key: Box Fill Calculations
   1. a. True
      The given square box has a maximum capacity of 21 in³ (344 cm³). As stated, the total count of conductors is nine 18-AWG conductors. Compare this number against the maximum number of conductors that is permitted for a box of this size.

      According to Table 314.16(A), this box is big enough for fourteen 18-AWG conductors. Therefore, the box has enough space for nine 18-AWG conductors.

   2. c. 26
      Go to Table 314.16(B) to find out the volume allowance for each conductor. According to the table, each 12-AWG conductor has a volume allowance of 2.25 in³.

      Next, divide the volume of the box by this volume allowance to get the maximum number of this type of conductor that can fit in the said box.

      $$N = 60\ in^3 \div 2.25\ in^3$$
      $$N = 26.67$$

      In this case, you cannot round up the number, so the maximum limit is 26 conductors.

   3. d. 32 cubic inches
      First, refer to Table 314.16(B) to calculate the volume allowance for all conductors, except the equipment grounding conductors.
      - *12-AWG conductors*
        *4 * 2.25 in³ = 9 in³*
      - *14-AWG conductors*
        *5 * 2.0 in³ = 10 in³*

Next, the single volume allowance for the cable clamps of the box should be made based on the largest conductor in the made.

Based on the earlier calculation, the largest conductor has a volume allowance of 2.25 in³. Therefore, the volume allowance for the clamps is also 2.25 in³.

For the devices—the 3-way switch and duplex receptacle outlet—each should get a double volume allowance based on the largest conductor that is connected to the device. Therefore:

- *3-way switch*
  *2 * 2 in³ = 4 in³*
- *Duplex receptacle outlet*
  *2 * 2.25 in³ = 4.5 in³*

A single volume allowance based on the largest equipment grounding conductor should be made if up to 4 equipment grounding conductors enter the box. In this case, the volume allowance for the equipment grounding conductor is 2.25 in³.

Your next step is to get the sum of the volume allowances of the conductors, clamps, devices, and equipment grounding conductors.

9 in³ + 10 in³ + 2.25 in³ + 4 + 4.5 in³ + 2.25 in³ = 32 in³

Based on this computation, the correct answer is 32 in³.

4. d. 4 x 2 1/8 square inches
   First, find out how many conductors of each size there are in the box.
   - 12 AWG = 6 conductors
     - 2 from the 12/2 NM cable
     - 1 from the cable clamp
     - 2 from the receptacle
     - 1 from the equipment grounding conductor
   - 14/3 NM = 5 conductors
     - 3 from the 14/3 NM cable
     - 2 from the switch

   Next, go to Table 314.16(B) to determine the volume of the conductors.

- 12 AWG

$$6 \text{ conductors} * 2.25 \text{ in}^3 = 13.50 \text{ in}^3$$

- 14 AWG

$$5 \text{ conductors} * 2 \text{ in}^3 = 10 \text{ in}^3$$

Get the sum of these two volumes to get the total volume of the conductors

$$13.50 \text{ in}^3 + 10 \text{ in}^3 = 23.50 \text{ in}^3$$

Lastly, refer to Table 314.16(A) to look for the appropriate electric box. Based on the requirement, the correct depth is 4 x 2 1/8 square inches.

5. b. 5 conductors
   The first thing to do is determine the count and size of the conductors that are currently in the box.
   - 12 AWG = 10 conductors
     o 4 from the two receptacles
     o 5 from 12-AWG conductors
     o 1 from the equipment grounding conductor

   Next, find out the volume of these conductors through Table 314.16(B).

$$10 \text{ conductors} * 2.25 \text{ in}^3 = 22.50 \text{ in}^3$$

Afterward, calculate the remaining space in the box for the 14-AWG conductors that will be added. Based on Table 314.16(A), the total space of the given box is 30.30 in³. You have to take into account the plaster ring, so the total space is 33.90 in³.

$$\text{Remaining Space} = \text{Total Space} - \text{Volume of the Existing Conductors}$$

$$\text{Remaining Space} = 33.90 \text{ in}^3 - 22.50 \text{ in}^3$$

$$\text{Remaining Space} = 11.40 \text{ in}^3$$

Finally, you can determine the number of additional 14-AWG conductors by dividing the remaining space by the volume of the additional conductor. According to Table 314.16(B), the 14-AWG conductor has a volume of 2 in³. Therefore:

11. $40 \text{ in}^3 \div 2 \text{ in}^3 = 5.70$

> *You cannot round up this number when doing box fill calculations, so the correct answer is 5 for the additional 14-AWG conductors.*

Conduit Fill Calculations

The Code specifies the requirements for conduit fill since improper practices can make an electrical installation dangerous to use. Failure to observe these rules would lead to rewiring works that tend to be expensive and time-consuming.

Given these, you must learn how to perform conduit fill calculations to pass the Journeyman Electrician Exam and to complete safe and proper installations in the field.

Before jumping ahead to the calculations, let's go over the basics first.

A conduit is a specific type of raceway. They serve as protection for cables so you need to select the appropriate material for the intended application. Some of the popular choices include:

- Electrical Metallic Tubing (EMT)
  This thin-walled conduit is normally used in areas that are not exposed to physical damage, such as above a suspended ceiling or within a hollow wall.

  A 1-inch EMT has the following specifications:
  - Wall Thickness: 1.4478 mm (0.057 in)
  - Outside Diameter: 29.5402 mm (1.163 in)
  - Internal Diameter: 26.6446 mm (1.049 in)
  - Internal Area: 556 mm² (0.864 in²)

- Intermediate Metal Conduit (IMC)
  The wall thickness and strength of this conduit lie somewhere between the EMT and RMC, hence its name. If approved, it can serve as an appropriate alternative for RMC.

  A 1-inch IMC has the following specifications:
  - Wall Thickness: 2.3622 mm (0.093 in)
  - Outside Diameter: 32.766 mm (1.29 in)

- Internal Diameter: 28.067 mm (1.105 in)
- Internal Area: 620 mm² (0.959 in²)

- Rigid Metal Conduit (RMC)
  Many consider this as the most widely used type of conduit for the installations of above-ground conduit systems. Common materials used for this type are aluminum or galvanized rigid steel.

  A 1-inch RMC has the following specifications:
    - Wall Thickness: 3.2004 mm (0.126 in)
    - Outside Diameter: 33.401 mm (1.315 in)
    - Internal Diameter: 27.0002 mm (1.063 in)
    - Internal Area: 573 mm² (0.887 in²)

- Rigid Nonmetallic Conduit (RNC) Schedule 40 PVC
  As the name indicates, this conduit is not made of metal. Instead, it is made of polyvinyl chloride or more commonly known as PVC. Compared to RMC, it has thicker walls. Applications of the Schedule 40 PVC type include underground installations for power and telephone.

  A 1-inch Schedule 40 PVC has the following specifications:
    - Wall Thickness: 3.6322 mm (0.143 in)
    - Outside Diameter: 33.401 mm (1.315 in)
    - Internal Diameter: 26.1366 mm (1.029 in)
    - Internal Area: 535 mm² (0.832 in²)

- Rigid Nonmetallic Conduit (RNC) Schedule 80 PVC
  This type of RNC has thicker walls than the Schedule 40 PVC. You can typically see this being used for risers that bring an underground electrical service up to a building or a transformer.

  A 1-inch Schedule 80 PVC has the following specifications:
    - Wall Thickness: 4.826 mm (0.19 in)
    - Outside Diameter: 33.401 mm (1.315 in)
    - Internal Diameter: 23.7744 mm (0.936 in)
    - Internal Area: 445 mm² (0.688 in²)

What can you find inside these conduits?

Again, depending on the intended application, the conduit fill consists of insulated wires or conductors. Matching the right kind of wire is also critical for the safety of the installation. Below are some of the most widely used conductors for different kinds of applications:

> **Remember!**
>
> For conduit fill calculations, the outside diameter, and wall thickness are not critical information. However, they can be used to calculate the internal diameter of the conduit, which is needed to determine the cross-sectional area of the conduit in case that the internal diameter of the conduit is not stated.
>
> The cross-sectional area of the wires, along with the number of cables and bends in the conduit are the factors that need to be considered when doing conduit fill calculations.

- THHN
  This conductor has a nylon jacket on its insulating material. Since it is rated $90^\circ C$ ($194^\circ F$) for both dry and damp locations, you may find this conductor in certain appliances and control circuits.

- THHW
  Rated $90^\circ C$ ($194^\circ F$) for dry locations and $75^\circ C$ ($167^\circ F$) for wet locations, this conductor is typically used for the feeders of permanent electrical installations. THHW has no outer coverings on its insulation.

- THWN
  Similar to THHN, this has a nylon jacket, too. Given that it is rated $75^\circ C$ ($167^\circ F$) for both dry and wet locations, it is more commonly used for general-purpose wiring and machine tools.

The conductor type that can be used for an installation is defined in the Code under the construction specifications. Whether the location is dry, damp, or wet also determines the type of conductor that will be used. For example, underground installations typically call for conductors that are rated for wet locations because the presence of underground water or moisture is quite likely.

Now that you are familiar with the materials for conduits and conductors, let's proceed to the calculation of the conduit size for the cable.

Three factors must be taken into consideration when doing conduit fill calculations:

a. The total number of cables in the conduit

b. The cross-section area of the cables
c. The total number of conduit bends

Based on these factors, you will be able to determine the capacity of a conduit for cables. They can also help you figure out the appropriate conduit size given the cables that you need to protect.

> **Take Note!**
>
> The maximum ratio for conduits and cables is affected by various factors, such as the type of application, as well as the number of cables and bends in the conduit. Chapter 9 of the NEC contains tables that serve as a reference when performing conduit fill calculations.

Examples of Conduit Fill Calculations

The various tables in Chapter 9 of the Code have reduced the amount of calculation that needs to be done while in the field. Using the right tables, you can find out the appropriate conduit size for your cables. To do that, follow the steps given below:

Step 1: Refer to Table 5 Dimensions of Insulated Conductors and Fixture Wires of NEC Chapter 9.

Step 2: Look up the type and size of the wires that you are going to use. You can find the insulation type of the wire on the first column, while the second column contains information about the size of the wire in AWG.

For this guide, let's say that you need to place a total of four 8-AWG THHN wires and two 4-AWG THW wires in an EMT conduit.

Step 3: Take note of the "Approximate Area" of each wire to be placed in the conduit.
The "Approximate Area" is expressed in square millimeters (mm^2) and square inches (in^2). This is the cross-sectional area of each wire.

For the example given above:

Insulation Type	Gauge	Approximate Area
THHN	8	23.61 mm^2 (0.0366 in^2)
THW	4	62.77 mm^2 (0.0973 in^2)

Step 4: Multiply the Approximate Area of each type of wire by the total number of the given wire that will be placed in the conduit.

As mentioned in Step 2, the conduit will have four 8-AWG THHN wires and two 4-AWG THW wires. Therefore:

$$(4 * 23.61 \text{ mm}^2) + (2 * 62.77 \text{ mm}^2) = 219.98 \text{ mm}^2$$

or

$$(4 * 0.0366 \text{ in}^2) + (2 * 0.0973 \text{ in}^2) = 0.341 \text{ in}^2$$

Based on the computation, the total cross-sectional area of the wires is 219.98 mm² (0.341 in²).

Step 5: Determine the minimum space available for the conduit. If you would look at Table 1 of Chapter 9, you will find the maximum fill for a conduit:

- One wire = 53%
- Two wires = 31%
- Three wires or more = 40%

Since the earlier example specifies a total of six wires, the maximum fill is 40% of the total space available of the EMT conduit. To get the minimum space available, multiply the total cross-sectional area of the wires by 40%.

$$219.98 \text{ mm}^2 * 40\% = 549.95 \text{ mm}^2$$

or

$$0.341 \text{ in}^2 * 40\% = 0.1364 \text{ in}^2$$

According to this computation, the minimum space available for your EMT conduit is 549.95 mm² (0.1364 in²).

Step 6: Refer to Table 4 in NEC Chapter 9.

Step 7: Look for the table that corresponds to the type of conduit that you are going to use.

Step 8: Check the column for "Over 2 Wires 40%" in the table for your conduit.
Look down the values listed in the column until you arrive at an area size that is greater than the computed minimum space available in Step 5.

For the earlier example, the conduit to be used is EMT. Since the minimum space available is 549.95 mm² (0.1364 in²), the EMT conduit must have at least be metric designator 53 (trade size 2). Any conduit size smaller than this would not be sufficient or safe for the six wires that are going to be placed within the said conduit.

You can also find out the maximum number of wires that you can run in a specific conduit using the NEC tables. Here's how:

Step 1: Refer to Table 4 of NEC Chapter 9.

Step 2: Look at the "Total Area 100%" column based on the type and size conduit you have.
Using the earlier example, the conduit type is EMT. The column you are looking for expresses the total area in square millimeters (mm²) and square inches (in²).
The total area of an EMT with a metric designator 53 (trade size 2) is 2,165 mm² (3.356 in²).

Step 3: Determine the total permissible wire fill.
Since you want to find out the maximum number of wires, the total area of the conduit must be multiplied by 40%, following Table 1 of NEC Chapter 9.

Therefore:

$$\text{Total Permissible Wire Fill} = 2{,}165 \text{ mm}^2 * 0.4 = 866 \text{ mm}^2$$

or

$$\text{Total Permissible Wire Fill} = 3.356 \text{ in}^2 * 0.4 = 1.3424 \text{ in}^2$$

You can also find these values for the total permissible wire fill in the columns under the header "Over 2 Wires 40%" of the table containing information about EMT.

Step 4: Refer to Table 5 of NEC Chapter 9.

Step 5: Check the "Approximate Area" of the type and size of wire that you want to place in the conduit.
The approximate area—also known as the cross-sectional area—is also expressed as square millimeters (mm^2) and square inches (in^2).

For this example, let's say that type of wire you intend to put inside the conduit is THWN (10 AWG) and RHH (1 AWG). The cross-sectional area for each 10-AWG THWN wire is 13.61 mm^2 (0.0211 in^2). Meanwhile, a 1-AWG RHH wire has a cross-sectional area of 122.6 mm^2 (0.1901 in^2)

Step 6: Add the approximate areas of each wire that will be placed in the conduit.
Stop adding when you reach the total permissible wire fill that you have computed in Step 3. You cannot exceed this so you would likely stop adding more wires before you can reach the said number.

Going back to the earlier example, you can fit a combination of twenty-seven 10-AWG THWN wires and four 1-AWG RHH wires in the EMT conduit with a total permissible wire fill of 866 mm^2 (1.3424 in^2) since the total wire area of this combination is only 857.87 mm^2 (1.3297 in^2). Look at the computation below to see how this ratio was determined:

13.61 mm^2 * 27 = 367.47 mm^2 or 0.0211 in^2 * 27 = 0.7479 in^2

122.6 mm^2 * 4 = 490.4 mm^2 or 0.1901 in^2 * 4 = 0.7604 in^2

The ratio of 10-AWG THWN wires to the 1-AWG RHH wires may be adjusted according to the intended application, provided that the total wire area of the two will not exceed the total permissible wire fill of the given EMT conduit.

Practice Questions: Conduit Fill Calculations

Instructions: Select the best answer from the given choices.

1. What should be the minimum RMC size if three 10-AWG THHN wires are going to be placed in it?
    a. metric designator 12 (trade size 3/8)

     b. metric designator 16 (trade size ½)
     c. metric designator 21 (trade size ¾)
     d. metric designator 27 (trade size 1)
2. How many 3-AWG XHHW wires can fit in a 1-inch Schedule 40 PVC conduit?
     a. one
     b. two
     c. three
     d. four
3. Determine the minimum conduit size for Schedule 80 PVC if there are three 500-kcmil XHHW wires and one 1/0-AWG XHHW wire.
     a. metric designator 78 (trade size 3)
     b. metric designator 91 (trade size 3 ½)
     c. metric designator 103 (trade size 4)
     d. metric designator 129 (trade size 5)
4. Find out how many 8-AWG THWN conductors can be placed in an EMT conduit with metric designator 16 (trade ½).
     a. one
     b. two
     c. three
     d. four
5. What is the minimum Schedule 40 PVC conduit size for five 4/0-AWG XHHW conductors?
     a. metric designator 35 (trade size 1 ¼)
     b. metric designator 41 (trade size 1 ½)
     c. metric designator 53 (trade size 2)
     d. metric designator 63 (trade size 2 ½)

Answer Key: Conduit Fill Calculations

1. b. metric designator 16 (trade size ½)

   To calculate the minimum RMC size for three 10-AWG THHN wires, you first need to get the total of the cross-sectional areas of the wires. You may find the information needed for this in Table 5 Dimensions of Insulated Conductors and Fixture Wires of NEC Chapter 9.

   According to the table, a 10-AWG THHN conductor has an approximate area of 13.61 mm² (0.0211 in²). Since there are three wires of this type

121

and size, the approximate area should be multiplied by 3, as depicted below:

$$13.61 \text{ mm}^2 * 3 = 40.83 \text{ mm}^2$$

or

$$0.0211 \text{ in}^2 * 3 = 0.0633 \text{ in}^2$$

Given that you have three wires, only 40% of the conduit fill can be used. Therefore, your next step is to multiply the total cross-sectional area of the wires by 40%.

$$40.83 \text{ mm}^2 * 40\% = 16.332 \text{ mm}^2$$

or

$$0.0633 \text{ in}^2 * 40\% = 0.15825 \text{ in}^2$$

Next, refer to the part of Table 4 that contains information about RMC. Look at the columns with the header "Over 2 Wires 40%", and search for the least value that is greater than the minimum conduit fill value that you have computed in the prior step.

Based on the table, the smallest size of the RMC given the conductors that would be placed in it is metric designator 16 (trade size ½).

2. c. three

First, let's assume that more than two XHHW can fit in the given conduit. Therefore, you can only use 40% of the conduit fill. Refer to Table 4 for the value you need, or multiply the total area of the conduit by 40%.

$$535 \text{ mm}^2 * 40\% = 214 \text{ mm}^2$$

or

$$0.832 \text{ in}^2 * 40\% = 0.333 \text{ in}^2$$

Your next step is to get the cross-sectional area of a 3-AWG XHHW wire. Refer to Table 5 for the value you are seeking. Based on the table, the approximate area for this conductor is 62.06 mm² (0.0962 in²).

To find out how many of these wires can safely fit in the conduit, divide the conduit fill you have computed earlier by the cross-sectional area of the wire.

$$214 \text{ mm}^2 / 62.06 \text{ mm}^2 = 3.4$$

or

$$0.33 \text{ in}^2 / 0.0962 \text{ in}^2 = 3.4$$

Given this, the maximum number of 3-AWG XHHW wires that the one-inch Schedule 40 conduit can fit is three.

3. a. metric designator 78 (trade size 3)
   The first thing you should do is get the total cross-sectional area of all the wires. Refer to Table 5 for the approximate area of each type:
   - 500-kcmil XHHW = 450.6 mm² (0.6984 in²)
   - 1/0-AWG XHHW = 117.7 mm² (0.1825 in²)

   Multiply the approximate area of the 500-kcmil XHHW by 3, and then add the approximate area of the 1/0-AWG XHHW.
   $$(450.6 \text{ mm}^2 * 3) + 117.7 \text{ mm}^2 = 1{,}469.5 \text{ } 117.7 \text{ mm}^2$$
   or
   $$(0.6984 \text{ in}^2 * 3) + 0.1825 \text{ in}^2 = 2.277 \text{ in}^2$$
   Next, look for the smallest value under the "Over 2 wires 40% columns" of the table for Schedule 80 PVC conduit that is more than the total cross-sectional area of the wires.

   Based on the table, the minimum conduit size is metric designator 78 (trade size 3).

4. b. two
   Given the size of the conduit, let's assume that its maximum limit is either one or two wires only. Looking at Table 4, the "1 Wire" column states 53% of the conduit fill of EMT is 104 mm² (0.161 in²). Meanwhile, the "2 Wires" column indicates that 31% of the conduit fill is 61 mm² (0.094 in²).

   Next, go to Table 5, and look up the approximate area of each 8-AWG THWN wire. According to the table, each wire has an approximate area of 23.61 mm² (0.0366 in²).

   While one 8-AWG THWN wire can safely fit in the EMT conduit, dividing the computed conduit fill for two wires by the approximate area of the THWN wire show that the EMT conduit can also safely fit two wires, but not three or more.
   $$61 \text{ mm}^2 / 23.61 \text{ mm}^2 = 2.5$$
   or
   $$0.094 \text{ in}^2 / 0.0366 \text{ in}^2 = 2.5$$

   Therefore, the answer is two 8-AWG THWN wires.

5. b. metric designator 41 (trade size 1 ½)
   Go to Table 5 for the approximate area of a 4/0-AWG XHHW wire, and multiply that value by 5 since five pieces of this conductor will be placed in the conduit.

   $$206.3 \text{ mm}^2 * 5 = 1{,}031.5 \text{ mm}^2$$
   or
   $$0.3197 \text{ in}^2 * 5 = 1.5985 \text{ in}^2$$

   Since there are more than 2 wires, look for the smallest value in the "Over 2 Wires" columns of Table 4 that are greater than the cross-sectional area of the five wires, or multiply the total of the approximate areas of the XHHW conductors.

   $$1{,}031.5 \text{ mm}^2 * 40\% = 412.6 \text{ mm}^2$$
   or
   $$1.5985 \text{ in}^2 * 40\% = 0.6394 \text{ in}^2$$

   Based on the table, the minimum conduit size that can fit five 4/0-AWG XHHW wires is metric designator 41 (trade size 1 ½).

Conductor Calculations

The Code specifies several requirements for conductor sizing and protection to prevent damages caused by overheating.

For example, Table 310.104(A) contains information about the properties of conductor insulation. In the table, you will find the lettering for common types of conductors with their corresponding operating temperatures, applications, as well as information about their insulation and outer covers.

Section 240.3, on the other hand, deals with the requirements for the protection of branch circuits, feeders, and service conductors based on their listed ampacities in Table 310.16.

Given that there are many applicable rules about conductor sizing and protection, this section will show how to do these calculations in preparation for the licensing exam.

Conductor Ampacity

This refers to the amount of current, as expressed in amperes, that a given conductor can carry continuously without going over the temperature rating indicated on its condition of use.

There are two ways to find out the conductor ampacity: through the Code, and an engineering formula. For the Journeyman Electrician Exam, you will have to rely on the first method. Table 310.16 of the NEC contains a list of allowable ampacities for conductors of different sizes. Take note that the ampacities included in this table are based on the temperature alone. Voltage drop is not considered because it is more relevant to efficiency but not the safety of the installation.

Moreover, Table 310.16 is made under the condition that only three or fewer current-carrying conductors are going to be placed together in a space with an ambient temperature of $30^{\circ}C$ ($86^{\circ}F$).

For example, the ampacity of a 6-AWG THHW copper conductor, rated $60^{\circ}C$, is 65 amperes. Meanwhile, a 1/0-AWG THHN aluminum conductor, rated $75^{\circ}C$, has an ampacity of 100 amperes.

Conductor Size

The Code expresses conductor sizes in AWG (American Wire Gauge). The commonly used sizes are from 18 AWG up to 4/0 AWG. Any conductor size beyond this range is measured in KCMILs (kilo circular mils).

In general, the minimum conductor size permitted for all occupancies is 14-AWG copper. However, the code also permits the usage of smaller conductors for certain locations or applications—for instance, motor control circuits and fixture wires.

The sizing of conductors must observe the temperature limits indicated in Table 310.15(B)(16). Using the conductor's ampacity, check the corresponding insulation rating and lowest temperature rating in the table.

For example, a circuit rated 50 amperes and has $60^{\circ}C$ terminals must have conductors that are not smaller than 6 AWG. Does that mean that an 8-AWG THHN insulated conductor ($90^{\circ}C$, rated 55 amperes for dry locations) can be used for this circuit? No, it can't be used at all because the terminal rating of $90^{\circ}C$ exceeds the $60^{\circ}C$ terminal rating of the circuit.

> **Interesting Fact**
>
> A bird can stand on a power line without getting electrocuted because it is touching only one power line at a time. However, if any part of the said bird touches another power line at the same time, it will be electrocuted because the bird's body will allow the electricity to flow, thus unintentionally creating an electric circuit.

When doing conductor sizing, you should also refer to Table 310.16 for the minimum size conductor. The table indicates terminal ampacities and the corresponding wire size for copper conductors if the terminal is rated 60°C or 75°C. For instance, the wire size for a terminal with an ampacity of 40 and a rating of 60°C is 8 AWG.

Conductor Protection

Information about the Code requirements for overcurrent protection of conductions can be found in Article 240. With the use of an overcurrent protective device, the circuit will not likely be damaged due to overheating because the device is triggered when a certain temperature level has been detected from the conductors. An overcurrent protective device has two ratings:

- Overcurrent Rating
  This refers to the actual ampere rating of the overcurrent protective device. If this rating is achieved, the circuit will be opened to prevent the excessive temperature from damaging the conductors or the insulation of the conductions.
- Ampere Interrupting Current (AIC) Rating
  The overcurrent protective device should have an AIC rating that is per the maximum fault current of the equipment to avoid extensive damage to its components.

To find out the required overcurrent protection for conductors, look at Table 310.15(B)(16). Take note of the permissions given in Section 240.4(A) to (G) as well.

For example, for overcurrent protective devices that are rated 800 amperes or lower, the next higher standard rating is permitted in as long as the overcurrent device rating is not more than 800 amperes, the conductors are not part of a branch circuit that supplies more than one receptacle for loads with cord-and-plug connections, and the ampacity of the conductor, after corrections and adjustments have been made, does not correspond with the standard ratings as stated in 240.6(A)

Practice Questions: Conductor Calculations

Instructions: Select the best answer from the given choices.

1. What should be the minimum size of THHN conductors for a circuit that is rated 50 amperes?
   a. 6 AWG

b. 8 AWG
   c. 12 AWG
   d. 18 AWG
2. If a 50-ampere circuit for a piece of equipment that is to be used at 75°C has THHN conductors, what must be the smallest size of the said conductors?
   a. 6 AWG
   b. 8 AWG
   c. 12 AWG
   d. 18 AWG
3. Determine the minimum size of THHN conductors that may be used for a 150-ampere feeder.
   a. 1/0 AWG
   b. 2/0 AWG
   c. 3/0 AWG
   d. 4/0 AWG
4. What should be the maximum size of the overcurrent protective device for 500-kcmil conductors that each have a rating of 380 amperes at 75°C and has a calculated load of 370 amperes?
   a. 200 amperes
   b. 400 amperes
   c. 600 amperes
   d. 800 amperes
5. What is the minimum conductor size for a 1,200-ampere feeder that runs in three parallel raceways?
   a. 250 kcmil
   b. 300 kcmil
   c. 400 kcmil
   d. 600 kcmil

Answer Key: Conductor Calculations

1. a. 6 AWG
   Refer to Table 310.15(B)(16)

2. b. 8 AWG
   Refer to Table 310.15(B)(16)

3. a. 1/0 AWG

Refer to Table 310.15(B)(16)

4. b. 400 amperes
   Refer to Table 310.15(B)(16)

5. d. 600 kcmil
   First, divide the ampere rating by the number of raceways.
   $Ampere\ per\ Parallel\ Conductor = 1,200\ amperes \div 3\ raceways$

   $Ampere\ per\ Parallel\ Conductor = 400\ amperes$

   Given this, refer to Table 310.16 to find out the correct conductor size. Based on the table, the conductor size should not be less than 600 kcmil.

Motor Calculations

For the electrician licensing exam, motor calculations cover a wide area ranging from designing motor circuits to protection motors in the event of a ground fault or short-circuit. As such, in this section, you will learn how to carry out motor calculations that you will encounter during the exam and while working in the field.

Motor Load

As discussed earlier, power refers to the amount of work done over a specific period. The power of a motor is typically based on its horsepower (HP).

One horsepower is equivalent to the amount of power required to move a load weighing 550 pounds by 1 foot in just 1 second. On the other hand, if you would speak of power in the electrical context, 1 HP is equal to 746 watts.

If a motor circuit has been designed according to the Code standards, then the motor will perform within the capacity according to its design and the motor circuit. The motor, as well as the motor circuit conductors, would also be protected from any damage that may be caused due to overload.

Before delving into the methods used for calculations involving motor circuits and overcurrent protection devices, you must first learn the basics of motor load.

The motor load refers to the device that loads a circuit. The greater the motor load, the higher the electrical current is going to be. Knowing what the motor load is would help you understand better how motor circuit conductors are sized.

A conductor is selected and used based on the maximum current that it can carry continuously without going over its temperature rating, as long as it operates under its condition of use. The sizing of wires depends on the load and the kind of environment where it will operate.

How can the Code help you comply with the safety standards that are related to the motor load?

- The NEC specifies the applicable parameters to general motor applications, and it states that for motors, the size of the conductors should be according to the allowable ampacity tables that are provided in 310.15(B).
- Moreover, 430.6 specifies the requirements for the ampacity of conductors and motor ratings. In 430.6(A)(1) and (A)(2) of the Code, you will also find the basis for the current rating for general motor applications.
- Table 430.247 contains information about the motor full-load current values that you need to determine the maximum current that conductors can carry in motor circuits.
- To determine the motor load of single-phase AC motors, check Table 430.248 Full-Load Currents in Amperes, Single-Phase Alternating-Current Motors.
- The full-load current values for two-phase AC motors are compiled in Table 430.249 Full-Load Current, Two-Phase Alternating-Current Motors (4-Wire).
- Meanwhile, Table 430.250 Full-Load Current, Three-Phase Alternating-Current Motors serves as the primary reference to find out

"A conductor is selected and used based on the maximum current that it can carry continuously without going over its temperature rating, as long as it operates under its condition of use. The sizing of wires depends on the load and the kind of environment where it will operate."

the full-load current of a 3-phase AC motor. You should not rely on the nameplate of the motor only.

To use those tables, look at the first column on the left-hand side of each table. In this column, the common values for the horsepower of motors are listed. On the other columns, you will find the full-load currents of motors that are permitted for different voltages.

For example, a single-phase, 1-HP, AC motor that operates at 200 volts has a full-load current of 9.2 amperes. In comparison, a two-phase, 1-HP AC motor has a full-load current of 3.2 amperes at 230 volts. The full-load current of a 3-phase, 1-HP AC motor with wound rotor and a voltage of 230 volts is 4.2 amperes.

These ampere ratings are the motor loads. This value is used when calculating the minimum allowable ampacity of conductors used for motor circuits. Now that you know where and how to find the correct full-load current of a given motor, let's proceed to motor circuit conductor calculations.

To calculate motor loads, you have to convert the current rating of the motor, as expressed in amperes, into its volt-amp rating. If the nameplate information is available, all you have to do is multiply the amperage as stated in the nameplate by the supply voltage.

Otherwise, you have to refer to the tables in NEC Article 430 for the current rating. Then, multiply the value you have obtained from the table by the supply voltage.

For example:

> What is the volt-amp rating for the following 3-phase motors, each running at 480 volts, if they are rated at 30 HP, 40 HP, and 125 HP respectively?
>
> Step 1: Refer to Table 430.150 for the FLA of each motor.
>
> > 30 HP = 40 amperes
> > 40 HP = 52 amperes
> > 125 HP = 156 amperes
>
> Step 2: Calculate the volt-ampere rating for each using this formula:
> $VA = 1.732 * V * I$ (where: VA = volt-ampere rating, V = voltage, A = ampere)

First Motor: 1.732 * 480 volts * 40 amperes = 33,254 VA
Second Motor: 1.732 * 480 volts * 52 amperes = 43,231 VA
Third Motor: 1.732 * 480 volts * 156 amperes = 129,692 VA

From the VA ratings of these motors, you can determine the total motor load by getting the sum of their VA ratings.

$Total\ Motor\ Load = 33,254\ VA + 43,231\ VA + 129,692\ VA$

$Total\ Motor\ Load = 206,177\ VA$

Let's take a look at another example of getting the total load if there are multiple loads on a single circuit.

In this instance, loads of the circuit consists of the following:

- 1st Load: 23-ampere HVAC unit
- 2nd Load: 40-ampere motor
- 3rd Load: 40-ampere lighting
- 4th Load: 52-ampere motor
- 5th Load: 65-ampere motor

What is the total load of this circuit?

Step 1: Get the sum of the given loads.

23 amperes + 40 amperes + 40 amperes + 52 amperes + 65 amperes = 220 amperes

Step 2: Add 25% of the largest load to the total.

This is based on the requirement stated in sections 430.6(A) and 430.24 of the Code.

Since the largest individual load is 65 amperes, multiply that number by 25%, and add the product to the total you have calculated in the previous step.

$(65\ amperes * 25) + 220\ amperes = 236.25\ amperes$

You can round up this number, so the total motor load for this circuit is 237 amperes.

Remember!

If any of the loads is a decimal number, round it up to the nearest whole number before getting the sum of all the loads.

Motor Conductors

To size the branch-circuit conductors of a motor, the Code explains that two conditions must be met:

a. In 210.19(A)(1), it states that the ampacity of the branch-circuit conductors cannot be of a smaller value than the maximum load that will be served after any adjustment or correction factor has been applied.
b. In 240.4, the Code requires the protection of branch-circuit conductors from overcurrent following the respective ampacities of the given conductors.

With these in mind, let's proceed to the sizing of the conductors for a single motor. According to the Code, the motor load should be based on the table, and the determined value must be multiplied by 125%. Then, use this value to look for the size of the conductor in the table.

For example, what size should the branch-circuit conductors be of a 7 ½-HP, 230-volt, 3-phase motor with terminals that are rated 60°C?

Step 1: Determine the full-load current of the motor.

Based on the table, the given motor has an FLA of 22 amperes.

Step 2: Compute the minimum rating of the conductors.

$Minimum\ rating = 22\ amperes * 125\%$

$Minimum\ rating = 27.5\ amperes$

Step 3: Refer to Table 310.15(B)(16) for the conductor size.

For this requirement, the conductor size should be 10 AWG, rated 30 amperes.

Sizing the conductors that supply more than one motor requires more effort. According to the 430.6(A) of the Code, the cables or feeders for this kind of setup must have a minimum ampacity of 125% of the full-load current rating of the motor with the highest rating, plus the sum of all the full-load current ratings of the other motors within the same group.

Let's go through the sample calculation of the minimum ampacity of the conductors based on this scenario:

The conductors are supplying one 5-HP, 415-volt, 3-phase motor, one 10-HP, 415-volt, 3-phase motor, one 15-HP, 415-volt, 3-phase motor, and one 5-HP, 230-volt, single-phase motor.

Step 1: Look up the full load current for each motor in the group.

- 5-HP, 415-volt, 3-phase motor = 7 amperes
- 10-HP, 415-volt, 3-phase motor = 13 amperes
- 15-HP, 415-volt, 3-phase motor = 19 amperes
- 5-HP, 230-volt, single-phase motor = 21 amperes

Step 2: Determine the minimum ampacity of the cables for the highest-rated motor.

Out of the motors in the group, the one with the highest capacity is the 15-HP, 415-volt, 3-phase motor. However, according to the table, the one with the highest full load current is the 5-HP, 230-volt, single-phase motor. As such, you should use it for the computation in this step.

$$Minimum\ rating = 21\ amperes * 125\%$$

$$Minimum\ rating = 26.25\ amperes$$

Step 3: Get the sum of the full-load currents of the other motors in the group and the minimum rating of the highest-rated motor.

Minimum Ampacity = 7 amperes + 12 amperes + 19 amperes + 26.25 amperes

$$Minimum\ ampacity = 65.25\ amperes$$

Step 4: Refer to Table 310.15(B)(16) for the appropriate conductor size for this group of motors.

Based on the table, the conductors for this requirement are 6 AWG, rated 75°C.

Motor Overload Protection

An overload protection device is needed to protect a motor from being damaged by heat when the said motor becomes loaded with too much work. Continuous duty motors with ratings that are greater than 1 HP must have an approved type of overload protection device. The Code also requires the installation of the device for every conductor that controls the operation of a motor that is rated more than 1 HP. Furthermore, the grounded leg of a 3-phase grounded system that is supplying a motor should also have an overload protection device—or an overcurrent device.

To size the overload protection device needed by a given motor, the full load current must be based on the ratings for the maximum and minimum set of an overload.

For the maximum overload, use this formula:

Maximum Overload = Full Load Current of the Motor* Allowable % of the Maximum Setting

An increase of 5% is allowed in case that the marked temperature is not more than 40^{0}C or the service factor is not lower than 1.15. Therefore, the allowable percentage of the maximum setting for motor overload protection is 130%.

> **Take Note!**
>
> Overload is not synonymous with a ground-fault or short-circuit. According to the Code, overload refers to the operating current that exceeds the allowable amount.

For the minimum overload, use this formula:

Maximum Overload = Full Load Current of the Motor * Allowable % of the Minimum Setting

The allowable percentage of the minimum setting for motors is 115%. However, an increase to 125% is also allowed, if the temperature rise does not exceed 40^{0}C or the minimum service factor is 1.15.

Short-Circuit and Ground-Fault Protection

According to Section 430.62, the feeder conductors of a motor must be protected against short-circuits or ground-faults through a protection device with a size that is not more than the largest rating of the short-circuit and ground-fault protective device for any motor, and the sum of all the full load currents of the motors within the same group.

To calculate the size, follow the steps given below.

For this example, the feeder protection is for one 20-HP, 460-volt, 3-phase motor, and one 10-HP, 460-volt, 3-phase motor It also has inverse-time breakers with 75°C terminals.

Step 1: Determine the full load current of each motor.

- 20-HP, 460-volt, 3-phase motor = 27 amperes
- 10-HP, 460-volt, 3-phase motor = 14 amperes

Step 2: Compute the largest branch-circuit protection device

- 20-HP, 460-volt, 3-phase motor

$$27\ amperes * 2.5 = 68\ amperes$$

According to the Code, the next size up should be used in this case so the correct answer is 70 amperes

- 10-HP, 460-volt, 3-phase motor

$$14\ amperes * 2.5 = 35\ amperes$$

Step 3: Add the largest protection device and the full load rating of the other motor.

$$70\ amperes + 14\ amperes = 84\ amperes$$

Based on the Code, you should use the next size down, so the correct size for the feeder protection is 80 amperes.

Practice Questions: Motor Calculations

Instructions: Select the best answer from the given choices.

1. What is the minimum rating for conductors that supply one 5-HP, 415-volt, 3-phase motor with a power factor of 0.8?
    a. 5.25 amperes
    b. 7.50 amperes
    c. 8.75 amperes
    d. 9.00 amperes
2. Size the conductors for a feeder of two 7 ½-HP, 230-volt, 3-phase motor.
    a. 2 AWG
    b. 4 AWG
    c. 6 AWG
    d. 8 AWG

135

3. The Code states that the minimum ampacity of a group of motors should be 125% of the full-load current rating of the motor with the highest capacity and the sum of the full-load current ratings of all other motors in the group.
    a. True
    b. False
4. What size of feeder protection would you need for one 5-HP, 230-volt, single-phase motor and one 3-HP, 230-volt, single-phase motor?
    a. 50-ampere inverse-time breaker
    b. 60-ampere inverse-time breaker
    c. 70-ampere inverse-time breaker
    d. 80-ampere inverse-time breaker
5. What should be the size of THW copper conductors if they are going to be used to supply a 60-ampere continuous load single-phase motor? Ten current-carrying conductors are placed in a single raceway, and the terminal ratings are all 75°C.
    a. 1 AWG
    b. 2 AWG
    c. 3 AWG
    d. 4 AWG

Answer Key: Motor Calculations

1. c. 8.75 amperes

   According to the table, the rating of the given 5-HP motor is 7 amperes. Therefore:

   $Minimum\ rating = 7\ amperes * 125\%$

   $Minimum\ rating = 8.75\ amperes$

2. d. 8 AWG

   Since the two motors have the same full load current, you can go ahead with the computation of the minimum rating of the conductors.

   $(22\ amperes * 125\%) + 22\ amperes = 49.5\ amperes$

   For this requirement, the table states that the conductor size should be 8 AWG.

3. b. False

The formula for the minimum ampacity requires 125% of the full-load current rating of the motor with the highest rating, not the motor with the highest capacity.

4. d. 80-ampere inverse-time breaker
    First, obtain the full load current of each motor from the table.
    - *5-HP, 230-volt, single-phase motor = 28 amperes*
    - *3-HP, 230-volt, single-phase motor = 17 amperes*

   Next, size the branch-circuit protected as required by the Code.

    - *5-HP, 230-volt, single-phase motor = 70 amperes*
    - *3-HP, 230-volt, single-phase motor = 45 amperes (next size up of 42.5 amperes)*

   Determine the size of the feeder conductor according to Section 430.24(A). Since the largest motor has a full load current of 28 amperes:

$$(28\ amperes * 125\%) + 17\ amperes = 52\ amperes$$

   According to Table 310.16, the smallest conductor for this requirement is 6-AWG, rated 55 amperes at 60^0C.

   Finally, size the feeder protection according to Section 430.62. The feeder protective device must not be more than the 70-ampere branch-circuit protection, plus the full load current of the other motor

$$70\ amperes + 17\ amperes = 87\ amperes$$

   The next size down from 87 amperes in the table is 80 amperes. Therefore, this is the size of the breaker that must be used for the given feeder.

5. a. 1 AWG
    First, determine the minimum rating of the conductors of the given motor.

$$Ampere\ rating = 60\ amperes * 125\%$$

$$Ampere\ rating = 75\ amperes$$

   Based on Table 310.15(B)(16), the THW conductor that can carry this requirement has a size of 4 AWG.

Next, divide the ampere rating of the conductor by 50% given that there are 10 current-carrying conductors in 1 raceway.

$Ampere\ rating\ =\ 60\ amperes * 50\%$

$Ampere\ rating\ =\ 120\ amperes$

Looking at Table 310.15(B)(16), 1-AWG conductors can carry this requirement at 75°C. Of the two sizes, the 1-AWG copper wire is larger so this is the correct answer.

Branch Circuit Calculations

In general, a branch circuit refers to the conductors that are in between the final overcurrent protection device of the circuit and the outlet. The Code covers different types of branch circuits, such as the appliance branch circuit, general-purpose branch circuit, and multi-wire branch circuit.

Part II of NEC 220 classifies three types of loads for branch-circuit calculations. First are the lighting loads for certain occupancies.

Table 220.12 contains information about the minimum sizes for lighting loads depending on the occupancy. For example, if the occupancy is a school, the minimum lighting load is 3 volt-amps per square foot. The table provides the minimum requirement, but for proper installation, the actual value may be exceeded.

For the calculation, you need to know the outside dimensions, in square feet, of the school. Afterward, just multiply the outside dimensions by 3 to get the total volt-amps for the lighting. This value will then be allocated across the required branch circuits to carry the said load.

> "And God said, 'Let there be light!', and there was light, but the Electricity Board said He would have to wait until Thursday to be connected."
>
> Spike Milligan

But what if the occupancy is not included in Table 220.12?

You have to refer to Section 220.14 for all occupancies not stated in the table, except if you are going to add loads to an existing installation. In that case, you have to refer to Section 220.16 instead.

Practice Questions: Branch Circuit Calculations

Instructions: Select the best answer from the given choices.

1. What must be the minimum ampacity of a tap conductor that supplies an industrial heater with a rating of 45 amperes?
    a. 10 amperes
    b. 20 amperes
    c. 30 amperes
    d. 40 amperes
2. Heavy-duty lamp holders must be connected to a branch circuit that has a minimum rating of:
    a. 10 amperes
    b. 20 amperes
    c. 30 amperes
    d. 40 amperes
3. What should be the ampere rating for a branch circuit that is permitted to supply a fixed lighting unit in any type of occupancy other than a dwelling unit?
    a. 10 amperes
    b. 20 amperes
    c. 30 amperes
    d. 40 amperes
4. For a 20-ampere, 240-volt branch circuit, what is the maximum continuous load that is permitted to be connected to it?
    a. 8 amperes
    b. 16 amperes
    c. 24 amperes
    d. 32 amperes
5. What is the calculated load of a branch circuit for a 12-kilowatt electric cooking range in a dwelling unit?
    a. 8 kilowatts
    b. 16 kilowatts
    c. 24 kilowatts

d. 32 kilowatts

Answer Key: Branch Circuit Calculations
1. b. 20 amperes
   Refer to 210.19(A)(4)

2. b. 20 amperes
   Refer to 210.21(A)

3. c. 30 amperes
   Refer to Table 310.15(B)(16)

4. d. 32 amperes
   According to the Code, a continuous load must have conductors that are rated 125% more than the connected load. Therefore:
   $Maximum\ Permitted\ Load = 20\ amperes * 125\%$
   $Maximum\ Permitted\ Load = 16\ amperes$

5. a. 8 kilowatts
   Based on Table 220.55, the calculated load should be 8 kilowatts because its nameplate rating is below 12 kilowatts.

Dwelling Load Calculations

Article 220 of the NEC contains the information you would need to perform calculations for residential occupancies. Details of the standard method of calculations can be found in Part II of the article, while an optional method is in Part III. Regardless of your choice of method, the Code specifies the minimum requirements only so these can be exceeded according to the design of the electrical work.

Load calculations for dwelling units differ depending on how many families reside in them. Therefore, in this section, we will tackle calculations for one-family dwelling units, and multifamily dwelling units.

One-Family Dwelling Units

Let's begin with the calculations under the standard method for feeder and service size calculations.

Step 1: Determine the total connected load.

To illustrate this, imagine a dwelling unit with a floor area of 2,000 square feet. According to Section 220.12, the load for the general lighting and receptacles for this occupancy is 3 VA per square foot. The dwelling unit also has a laundry circuit and two small-appliance circuits—all of which have a rating of 1,500 VA each. Therefore:

- General lighting and receptacles load

$$2,000\ square\ feet * 3\ VA = 6,000\ VA$$

- Laundry circuit load

$$1,500\ VA * 1 = 1,500\ VA$$

- Small-appliance circuits load

$$1,500\ VA * 2 = 3,000\ VA$$

Get the sum of these loads to determine the total connected load.

$$Total\ Connected\ Load = 6,000\ VA + 1,500\ VA + 3,000\ VA$$

$$Total\ Connected\ Load = 10,500\ VA$$

Apply the demand factor, as specified in Table 220.42, to the total connected load. According to the Code, the circuits for general lighting and receptacle, small appliances, and laundry are not going to be operated simultaneously at full load. Therefore, the demand factor can be applied right away to the total connected load.

For dwelling units, the first 3,000 VA must be calculated at 100% demand, while the remainder should be at 35%. Therefore:

$$Total\ Demand\ Load = (3,000\ VA * 100\%) + (7,500\ VA * 35\%)$$

$$Total\ Demand\ Load = 3,000\ VA + 2,625\ VA$$

$$Total\ Demand\ Load = 5,625\ VA$$

Step 2: Apply the demand factors for appliances circuits.

Based on Section 220.17 of the Code, a demand factor of 75% may be used if there are four or more

Remember!

The floor area should be based on the dwelling unit's outside dimensions. However, it should not include the garage, open porch, or any spaces that cannot be used or finished in the future.

appliances fastened in place are on the same feeder within a dwelling unit. Examples of such appliances are a dishwashing unit, electric waste disposal equipment, and a trash compactor.

Here is a sample calculation of the total connected appliance load if the 2,000-square-feet dwelling unit described above has the following nameplate ratings:
- Dishwashing equipment (1,200 VA)
- Electric trash compactor (1,100 VA)
- Waste disposal equipment (900 VA)
- Water Heater (4,500 VA)

Get the sum of these appliance nameplate ratings to find out the total connected appliance load.

$$1,200\ VA + 1,100\ VA + 900\ VA + 4,500\ VA = 7,700\ VA$$

Next, apply the demand factor of 75% to the total connected load of the appliances.

$$Total\ Connected\ Appliance\ Load\ =\ 7,700\ VA * 75\%$$

$$Total\ Connected\ Appliance\ Load\ =\ 5,775\ VA$$

Step 3: Determine the dryer calculated load for the dwelling unit.

Section 220.54 of the NEC states that the feeder or service load for a clothes dryer in a dwelling unit must at least be 5,000 watts. However, in the case that the rating on the nameplate of the equipment is greater than 5,000 watts, the nameplate rating should be used.

Let's say that in the given dwelling unit in the previous steps, there is one clothes dryer that has a rating of 4,000 watts with a voltage system of 120/240 volts. Based on the requirements stated by the code, the dryer demand load for this clothes dryer is 5,000 watts.

Step 4: Determine the demand load of cooking equipment.

Demand factors can be applied to cooking equipment in dwelling units with ratings that are higher than 1,750 watts, as specified in Table 220.55 and the following Informational Notes 1, 2, and 3.

In the dwelling unit from the previous steps, the following household cooking appliances are being used by the residents:

Important!

If the dwelling unit has more than 4 clothes dryers in it, the demand factors in Table 220.54 may be applied. On the other hand, if the dwelling unit has no clothes dryer in it, then you are not required to consider the feeder or service dryer load for the said dwelling unit.

- Cooktop (1 unit at 6,000 VA)
- Oven (2 units at 3,000 VA each)

The calculation for the demand loads of each type of equipment should be like this:

- Cooktop

$6,000\ VA * 1\ unit * 80\% = 4,800\ watts$

- Oven (2 units at 3,000 VA each)

$3,000\ VA * 2\ unit * 75\% = 4,500\ watts$

Next, get the sum of the two demands.

$Total\ Demand\ Load = 4,800\ watts + 4,500\ watts$

$Total\ Demand\ Load = 9,300\ watts$

Step 5: Determine the air conditioning and heating loads.

According to Section 220.60, since the loads for the air conditioning and the heating in a dwelling unit are not turned on at the same time, the load with the lesser value may be omitted. Still, the applicable demand factor for both of these loads is at 100%

Let's go over an example of how to calculate the loads for a dwelling occupancy with 3 space heating units, each rated at 3,000 watts, and a 5-HP air conditioning unit with a voltage of 230 volts.

To calculate the VA rating of the space heaters:

$VA = 3,000 \, watts * 3 \, units$

$VA = 9,000 \, watts$

For the air conditioning unit, refer to Table 430.248 and follow this formula:

$VA = Voltage * Current$

$VA = 230 \, volts * 17 \, amperes$

$VA = 3,910 \, VA$

Given that the load of the air conditioning unit is smaller than that of the heating load, the air conditioning load may be omitted.

Step 6: Size the service and feeder conductors.

One-family dwellings use a 120/240-volt system to supply the service and feeder conductors. Section 310.15(B)(7)(1) to (4) can be used to size the service and feeder conductors of dwelling units. Here are some important points to note when doing this step:

> **Reminder!**
> For the calculation of neutral loads for electric cooking equipment and clothes dryers in dwelling units, use a demand factor of 70%, as stated in Section 220.55.

- Section 310.15(B)(7) does not apply to feeder conductors that are connected to a 3-phase 120/280-volt system, or a 3-wire service. Even if the load on the phases is balanced, the conductors in the said systems carry the neutral current.
- The ampacity of service conductors that supply a whole load of a one-family dwelling unit is 83% of the service rating.
- Unless permitted in Section 310.15(B)(7)(3), sizing feeder conductors cannot be performed according to 310.15(B)(7)(2) where the said feeder does not carry a full load of a dwelling unit.

For this calculation, get the total demand load from the previous steps and then apply this formula:

$I = VA \div E$

Where:

> I = current
> VA = total demand load in volt-amperes
> E = voltage

$I = 29,700\ VA \div 240\ volts$

$I = 124\ amperes$

According to Table 310.15(B)(16), the sizing for the feeder/service conductors of this dwelling unit is 130-ampere service with 1-AWG conductors.

Now that you know how to the standard method, let's try the optional method using the same example of a dwelling from the previous approach. Take note that the optional method can only be used for dwelling units that are being served by any of the following:

- 120/240-volt system
- 120/280-volt system
- 3-wire service or feeder conductors with a minimum ampacity of 100 amperes

The optional method is quicker to perform compared to the standard method, as you will observe in the steps given below.

Step 1: Determine the general loads of the dwelling unit.

For this step, observe the following requirements as specified by the Code:

- General Lighting and Receptacles – 3 VA per square foot
- Small-Appliance Circuit – 1,500 VA per 20-ampere circuit
- Laundry Circuit – 1,500 VA per 20-ampere circuit
- Appliances – nameplate ratings of all permanently connected appliances or those fastened in place on the same circuit.

The first 10,000 VA should be calculated at 100%, while the remained should be at 40%. Therefore, based on the computed loads of the 2,000-square-feet dwelling unit earlier:

$Calculated\ General\ Load = 10,500\ VA + 7,700\ VA + 4,000\ VA + 9,300\ VA$

$Calculated\ General\ Load = (10,000\ VA * 100\%) + (21,500 * 40\%)$

$Calculated\ General\ Load\ =\ 18,600\ VA$

Step 2: Determine the air conditioning or heating load.

Consider only the larger load of the following loads, based on the requirements indicated in Section 220.82(C)(1) to (6):

- Air conditioning/cooling equipment
  100% of the nameplate rating
- Heat-pump without electric heating supplement
  100% of the nameplate rating
- Heat-pump compressor with electric heating supplement
  For the compressor, 100% of its nameplate rating. For the supplement, 65% of its rating. However, if the compressor cannot operate at the same time as the supplement, then it may be omitted.
- Electric space heating with less than 4 units that have separate controls
  65% of the nameplate rating
- Electric space heating with four or more units that have separate controls
  40% of the nameplate rating
- Electric thermal storage and other types of electric heating systems
  100 of the nameplate rating

Based on the air conditioning and heating equipment of the 2,000-square-feet dwelling unit, the larger of the two loads is from the space heaters. Applying the requirements given above, the heating load for this calculation should be multiplied by 65% since it has 3 separately controlled units.

$9,000\ VA\ *\ 65\%\ =\ 5,850\ VA$

Step 3: Size the feeder/service conductors of the dwelling unit.

First, add the calculated general load to the heating load:

$Total\ Calculated\ Load\ =\ 18,600\ VA\ +\ 5,850\ VA$

$Total\ Calculated\ Load\ =\ 24,450\ VA$

Next, apply this formula for current:

$$I = VA \div E$$

Where:

I = current
VA = volt-ampere
E = voltage

> **Did You Know That...**
>
> About half of the total electricity bill of an average family in the US comes from the usage of air cooling or space heating appliances? Lighting only takes up a small fraction of the electricity bill, especially with the introduction of LED light bulbs for homes. Compared to their traditional counterparts, an LED light bulb only needs 1/6 of the power that a conventional light bulb of the same wattage requires.

$$I = 24,450\ VA \div 240\ volts$$

$$I = 102\ amperes$$

Refer to Table 310.16 for the sizing of the feeder/service conductor. For this calculation, the size should be 110-ampere service with 3-AWG conductors.

Multifamily Dwelling Units

A multifamily dwelling unit consists of three or more dwelling units. Compared to one-family dwelling units that tend to use nonmetallic cables, multifamily dwelling uses raceways and cables that are made of metal.

In terms of sizing feeder or service of multifamily dwelling, you need to refer to Section 310.15(B)(16). However, for a single dwelling unit within a multifamily dwelling Section 310.15(B)(7) may be used as long as the multifamily dwelling uses a 120/240-volt single-phase system.

Much like one-family dwelling units, calculations for the feeder or service size can be done through the standard method and the optional method. The main difference is the demand factors that should be used for multifamily structures.

Let's take a look at this example, and use the two methods to see how the calculation should go.

Think of a 10-unit multifamily dwelling building, where each unit has a floor area of 1,000 square feet. Each unit has 2 small-appliance circuits and 1 laundry circuit. For appliances, every unit has one 4.5-kilowatt water heater, one 1,200-VA dishwasher, one 900-VA electric waste disposal equipment, one 5.5-kilowatt clothes dryer, one 10-kilowatt 120/240-volt cooking equipment, one 5-HP 240-volt air conditioning unit, and one 6.0-kilowatt 240-volt space heater.

Using the standard method:

> Step 1: Determine the total connected load of the 10 dwelling units in the multifamily dwelling building.
>
> Like in the one-family dwelling calculation, the load for general lighting and receptacles should be 3 VA per square foot.

Take Note!

According to Exception No. 1 of NEC Section 210.52(F), you do not have to add a laundry circuit for each unit in a multifamily dwelling structure if it has a shared laundry area for all units instead.

> Meanwhile, each small-appliance circuit and laundry circuit should be 1,500 VA.
>
> - General Lighting and Receptacle

$$3\ VA * 1,000\ square\ feet = 3,000\ VA$$

> - Small-Appliance Circuits

$$1,500\ VA * 2\ circuits = 6,000\ VA$$

> - Laundry Circuit

$$1,500\ VA * 1\ circuit = 1,500\ VA$$

> Next, get the sum of these loads and multiply it by 10 units to determine the total connected load.

$$Total\ Connected\ Load = (3,000\ VA + 6,000\ VA + 1,500\ VA) * 10\ units$$

$$Total\ Connected\ Load = 75,000\ VA$$

> According to Table 220.42, the demand factor for the first 3,000 VA is 100%. VA ranging from 3,0001 to 120,000 should be at 35%, while the remainder—120,001 VA and upwards—should be at 25%. Therefore:

$$Total\ Demand\ Load = (3,000\ VA * 100\%) + (72,000\ VA * 35\%)$$

$$Total\ Demand\ Load = 28,200\ VA$$

> Step 2: Determine the demand load of the appliances.

Except for clothes dryers, cooking equipment, air conditioning equipment, or space heating equipment, a demand factor of 75% may be applied when 4 or more appliances are fixed on the main service.

For multifamily dwelling calculations, all appliances in all units must be taken into account. Looking back at the example, get first the sum of the demand loads of the dishwasher, electric waste disposal equipment, and water heater.

$1,200\ VA + 900\ VA + 4,500\ watts = 6,600\ VA$

Next, multiply the sum by 10 units and then apply the demand factor.

$Appliance\ Demand\ Load = (6,600\ VA * 10\ units) * 75\%$

$Appliance\ Demand\ Load = 49,500\ VA$

Step 3: Compute the total load of the clothes dryers in each unit. Perform this step only if the individual dwelling unit has a clothes dryer. Otherwise, this computation cannot be used for common laundry facilities of a multifamily dwelling structure.

The Code states that the load must at least be 5,000 watts. If the nameplate rating is higher, then that must be used in the calculation. Based on the earlier scenario, every unit has a 5.5-kilowatt clothes dryer. Multiply this by 10 units and then apply the demand factor, as listed in Table 220.54.

$Dryer\ Demand\ Load = (5,500\ watts * 10\ units) * 50\%$

$Dryer\ Demand\ Load = 27,500\ watts$

Step 4: Obtain the demand load of the cooking equipment of all units. The demand factors in Table 220.55—including Informational Notes 1, 2, and 3—can be applied if the cooking equipment has a rating that is greater than 1 ¾ kilowatt.

Since the equipment provided for each unit in the multifamily dwelling building is rated 10.0 kilowatts, you can compute the demand load by multiplying the equipment load by 10 units and by the applicable demand factor.

$$Cooking\ Equipment\ Demand\ Load = (10,000\ watts * 10\ units) * 25\%$$

$$Cooking\ Equipment\ Demand\ Load = 25,000\ watts$$

> Step 5: Determine whether the air conditioning load or the heating load would be considered in the calculation.
> The smaller value of the two should be omitted.
> - Air Conditioning Unit

$$VA = [240\ volts * (16.70\ amperes + 1.20\ amperes)] * 10\ units$$

$$VA = 43,000\ VA$$

> - Space Heater

$$VA = 6,000\ watts * 10\ units$$

$$VA = 60,000\ watts$$

> The load of the space heaters is greater than that of the air conditioning equipment. Therefore, the latter should be omitted.

> Step 6: Size the feeder and service conductor.

> First, get the total of all the loads that you have computed in all the previous steps.

> Total Connected Load = 28,200 VA + 49,500 VA + 27,500 watts + 25,000 watts + 60,000 watts

$$Total\ Connected\ Load = 190,200\ VA$$

> Refer to Table 310.15(B)(16) for the appropriate conductor size given the total connected load.

Having learned the standard method, let's proceed with the optional method as described in Part IV of Article 220. For multifamily dwelling units, refer to Section 220.84 for the demand factors that must be applied. The demand factors listed in Table 220.84 are based on the number of dwelling units.

Before going through the sample calculation, keep in mind that the optional method can only be done if:

- The multifamily dwelling structure has three or more dwelling units in it
- Each dwelling unit within the multifamily dwelling structure is supplied by only one feeder and comes with cooking equipment
- The feeder is assigned to dwelling units with air conditioning or electric space heating

For house loads like the lighting in the lobby and parking lot of the multifamily dwelling structure, their loads must be calculated separately, and then added to the total demand load that you would obtain through the following steps:

Step 1: Determine the total connected load.

Get the sum of the connected loads from each unit in the multifamily dwelling before applying the demand factor in Table 220.84.

- General lighting and receptacles
    - 3 VA per square foot
    - $3\ VA * 1,000\ square\ feet * 10\ units = 30,000\ VA$
- Small-appliance circuits
    - 1,500 VA per circuit, with a minimum of 2 circuits per unit
    - $1,500\ VA * 2\ circuits * 10\ units = 30,000\ VA$
- Laundry circuits
    - 1,500 VA per circuit, only if each unit has its laundry equipment
    - $1,500\ VA * 1\ circuit * 10\ units = 15,000\ VA$
- Appliance circuits
    - Nameplate rating of every appliance in all units
    - (1,200 V A + 900 V A + 4,500 watts) * 10 units = 66,000 V A
- Cooking equipment
    - Nameplate rating of every cooking equipment in all units
    - $10,000\ watts * 10\ units = 100,000\ watts$
- Clothes Dryers

> **Important!**
>
> In case that other loads must be considered, such as those in common areas, lobbies, and parking lots, calculate their loads separately according to the requirements stated in Part III of Article 220. Add the computed loads to the total connected load before sizing the conductor of the feeder and service.

- Nameplate rating of every clothes dryer in all units, unless the dryers are in the shared laundry facility of the multifamily dwelling building
- $5,500\ watts * 10\ units = 55,000\ watts$
- Air Conditioning or Heating
  - A load of whichever is higher of the two
  - 60,000 watts (space heating) because the load of the air conditioner is only 43,000 watts

To get the total connected load, just add up all of these loads.

Total Connected Load + 30,000 V A + 30,000 V A + 15,000 V A + 100,000 watts + 55,000 watts + 60,000 watts

$Total\ Connected\ Load = 290,000\ VA$

Step 2: Apply the demand factor.

Go to Table 310.15(B) for the appropriate demand factor for the total connected load from the previous step.

Step 3: Size the feeder and service conductors.

Sizing conductors for multifamily dwelling structures require feeders to be based on the demand load of all the individual dwelling units within the structure. Here are some important points to keep in mind during this step:

- If the demand load—calculated using the standard method—for two individual dwelling units that are receiving supply from the same feeder is more than the value calculated using the optional method, the load with the lesser value may be used.
- The neutral load, as indicated in Part III of Article 220, refers to the maximum unbalanced load between the neutral conductor and an ungrounded conductor.
- The neutral demand load of electric cooking equipment should be calculated at 70% of the demand load.

For feeders or service conductors, you may use Section 310.15(B)(7) as a reference for 120/240-volt single-phase systems. However, for the conductors that feed the said service, Table 310.15(B)(16) should be used instead.

Practice Questions: Dwelling Load Calculations

Instructions: Select the best answer from the given choices.

1. If the total connected load of a one-family dwelling unit is 12,000 VA, what is its calculated demand load?
    a. 3
    b. 6
    c. 9
    d. 12
2. For a dwelling unit, what is the minimum load for a laundry circuit?
    a. 1,200 VA
    b. 1,500 VA
    c. 1,800 VA
    d. 2,100 VA
3. What is the total demand load for the dryer circuits of an 8-unit multifamily dwelling building, where every unit has a 5,000-watt clothes dryer?
    a. 12,000 watts
    b. 24,000 watts
    c. 36,000 watts
    d. 48,000 watts
4. What is the demand load of the feeder for a 230-volt dwelling unit that has a 30-ampere air conditioner, and three 3,000-watt space heaters?
    a. 3,000 watts
    b. 6,000 watts
    c. 9,000 watts
    d. 12,000 watts
5. What is the appliance demand load if a dwelling unit has four appliances that are fixed in place, and each appliance is rated 800 VA?
    a. 2,120 VA
    b. 2,240 VA
    c. 2,360 VA
    d. 2,480 VA

6. What is the calculated demand load for a 15-unit multifamily dwelling building, where each unit has a floor area of 900 square feet?
    a. 3,000 VA
    b. 108,000 VA
    c. 36,750 VA
    d. 39,750 VA

7. Determine the total demand load of a 1,250-square-feet one-family dwelling unit that has the following loads:
    - Air Conditioner – 2,500 VA
    - Cooking Range – 5,000 VA
    - Dishwasher – 1,400 VA
    - Dryer – 5,000 VA
    - Laundry Machine – 1,500 VA
    - Space Heater – 3,000 VA
    - Waste Disposal Equipment – 1,000 VA
    - Water Heater – 1,200 VA

   Use the standard method for your calculation.

    a. 10,118 VA
    b. 15,118 VA
    c. 20,118 VA
    d. 25,118 VA

8. A 12-unit multifamily building is being supplied by a 120/240-volt single-phase system. Each unit has a floor area of 1,500 square feet, and contains the following equipment and corresponding loads:
    - Air Conditioner – 3,900 VA (230 volts, 17 amperes)
    - Cooking Range – 14,400 VA
    - Dishwasher – 1,500 VA
    - Dryer – 4,500 VA
    - Laundry Machine – 1,200 VA
    - Space Heater – 5,000 VA
    - Water Heater – 4,000 VA

   Using the optional method, what should be the conductor size if the rating of the service is 120/240-volt single-phase system, and two parallel raceways are used for the conductors?

    a. 300-AWG conductors rated 700 amperes
    b. 300-kcmil conductors rated 450 amperes
    c. 600-AWG conductors rated 800 amperes

d. 600-kcmil conductors rated 420 amperes

Answer Key: Dwelling Load Calculations

1. a. 3

    Refer to 220.42 for the applicable demand factors.

    $Calculated\ Demand\ Load = (12,000\ VA - 3,000\ VA) * 35\%$

    $Calculated\ Demand\ Load = 3,150\ VA$

2. c. 1,800 VA

    Refer to 220.52(B)

3. b. 24,000 watts

    To calculate the total dryer demand load, multiply the total connected load by its demand factor, as stated in 220.54:

    $Total\ Demand\ Load = (8\ units * 5,000\ watts) * 60\%$

    $Total\ Demand\ Load = 24,000\ watts$

4. c. 9,000 watts

    First, compute the rating of the air conditioner:

    $30\ amperes * 230\ volts = 6,900\ VA$

    Next, determine the load of the three space heaters:

    $3\ units * 3,000\ watts = 9,000\ watts$

    Between the two loads, the demand load of the heaters is higher than that of the air conditioner. Therefore, the latter should be omitted, and only the heater load will be considered.

5. b. 2,240 VA

    According to the Code, the total demand load if there are four or more appliances that are fixed in place is 70% of the total load. Therefore:

    $Appliance\ Demand\ Load = (4\ units * 800\ VA) * 70\%$

    $Appliance\ Demand\ Load = 2,240\ VA$

6. d. 39,750 VA

First, compute the total loads per unit:
- General Lighting and Receptacle Load

$3\ VA * 900\ square\ feet = 2,700\ VA$

- Small-Appliances Load

$1,500\ VA * 2\ circuits = 3,000\ VA$

- Laundry Load

$1,500\ VA * 1\ circuit = 1,500\ VA$

Get the sum of these loads, and then multiply by 15 units:
$(2,700\ VA + 3,000\ VA + 1,500\ VA) * 15\ units = 108,000\ VA$

To determine the total demand load of all units in the multifamily dwelling building:
$Total\ Demand\ Load = (3,000\ VA * 100\%) + (105,000\ VA * 35\%)$

$Total\ Demand\ Load = 39,750\ VA$

7. c. 6,000 VA

   To find out the total connected load:
   - *General Lighting and Receptacle Load*

$3\ VA * 1,250\ square\ feet = 3,750\ VA$

   - *Small-Appliances Load*

$1,500\ VA * 2\ circuits = 3,000\ VA$

   - *Laundry Load*

$1,500\ VA * 1\ circuit = 1,500\ VA$

   Get the sum of these loads and multiply by the demand factor.

$(3,000\ VA * 100\%) + (4,050\ VA * 35\%) = 4,418\ VA$

   For the appliance load:

$(1,400\ VA + 1,000\ VA + 1,200\ VA) * 75\% = 2,700\ VA$

   For the dryer load: 5,000 VA

   For the cooking load: 5,000 VA

156

For the air conditioning or heating load: 3,000 VA, because the air conditioning load is smaller and thus it can be omitted from the calculation

Get the sum of these computed loads to obtain the answer:

Total connected Load = 4,418 V A + 2,700 VA + 5,000 VA + 5,000 VA + 3,000 VA

$Total\ Connected\ Load\ =\ 20,118\ VA$

8. d. 600-kcmil conductors rated 420 amperes
   First, determine the total connected load of all units.
   - *General Lighting and Receptacles Load*

$3\ VA\ *\ 1,500\ square\ feet\ =\ 4,500\ VA$

   - *Small-Appliances Load*

$1,500\ VA\ *\ 2\ circuits\ =\ 3,000\ VA$

   - *Laundry Load*

$1,500\ VA\ *\ 1\ circuit\ =\ 1,500\ VA$

   - *Appliance Load*

$14,400\ VA\ +\ 1,500\ VA\ +\ 4,500\ VA\ +\ 4,000\ VA\ =\ 24,400\ VA$

   - *Air Conditioning/Heating Load*
     o *Air Conditioning Load = 3,910 VA*
     o *Heating Load = 5,000 VA*
     Omit the air conditioning load from the calculation

     *Total Connected Load = (4,500 V A + 3,000 V A +1,500 V A + 24,400 V A + 5,000 V A * 12 units*

$Total\ Connected\ Load\ =\ 460,800\ VA$

Next, apply the demand factor.

$Total\ Calculated\ Load\ =\ 460,800\ VA\ *\ 41\%$

$Total\ Calculated\ Load\ =\ 188,928\ VA$

To determine the conductor size, use the formula $I = VA \div E$

$I = 188,928\ VA \div 240\ volts$

$I = 787\ amperes$

Since the conductors are installed in two parallel raceways, the current should be divided by 2.

$787\ amperes \div 2\ raceways = 383\ amperes$

Based on the table, service conductors with the size of 600 kcmil, rated 420 amperes would be enough to meet the given load requirements of the multifamily dwelling building.

Commercial Load Calculations

Information related to commercial load calculations can be found mostly in Article 220 of the NEC, though some important relevant requirements can be found in other parts of the Code. This is the challenging aspect of doing load calculations for commercial buildings, such as offices, restaurants, and warehouses. You have to be familiar with the requirements for the different types of occupancies, as well as the unique rules that need to be applied for their feeders and service loads.

Here are some tips that could help you with commercial load calculations:

- Refer to Table 220.3 for information about branch-circuit calculations for specific equipment.
- Nominal system voltages must be used for calculations of branch circuits, feeders, and service loads, except when the given scenario specifies a different voltage.

> "We believe that electricity exists because the electric company keeps sending us bills for it, but we cannot figure out how it travels inside wires."
>
> Dave Barry

- If the value of an ampere is not a whole number, you can round up to the nearest whole number if the decimal is 0.50 or higher. On the other hand, decimals below 0.50 can be dropped.
- The floor area of a commercial occupancy must be calculated according to its outside dimensions.

Specific Loads

NEC Article 220 has most of the information that you would need to calculate the specific loads of commercial occupancies. For example:

- Commercial Kitchen Equipment
    - The branch-circuit conductors and overcurrent protection devices must be sized according to the nameplate rating of the kitchen equipment.
    - Calculation of the service demand loads for kitchen equipment that are used intermittently or has thermostatic controls should consider the demand factors in Table 220.20, and apply them to the total load of the connected kitchen equipment.
    - The feeder load cannot be less than the total of the two largest appliance loads.
    - Similarly, service demand loads cannot be less than the sum of the loads of the two largest appliances.
    - The demand factors in Table 220.20 are not applicable for equipment used for ventilation, air-conditioning, or area heating.
- Commercial Laundry Machine
    - The sizing of its circuits is based on the nameplate rating.
    - If the machine is not a continuous load, then you can assume that the rating is 1,500 VA, unless a different rating is stated.
- Commercial Dryers
    - The sizing of the branch-circuit conductors and overcurrent protection device should be based on the nameplate rating.
    - The feeder demand load is calculated at 100%.
    - If the dryer is operated continuously, the sizing of the branch-circuit conductor and overcurrent protection device should be at 125% of the load.
    - The demand factors in Table 220.18 are not applicable for commercial dryers.
- Lighting

- Though the Code sets a minimum load per square foot for lighting, the value varies depending on the occupancy type.
- For the demands factors applicable to lighting equipment of hospitals, warehouses, and guestrooms of hotels and motels, refer to Table 220.11.
- If the lighting loads for the said types of occupancies are continuous, the value of the general lighting load stated in Table 220.11 should be multiplied by 125%.

Receptacle Loads

Calculations for receptacle load depend on the requirements for the different applications, as stated in the Code.

- Maximum Number of Permitted Receptacles per Circuit
    - This calculation should be based on the ampacity of the circuit.
    - To determine the maximum number, divide the VA rating of the given circuit by each strap. A receptacle strap has a rating of 180 VA.
- Sizing of Receptacles
    - In general, circuits with a minimum rating of 15 amperes are permitted by the Code for commercial occupancies.
- Receptacle VA Load
    - Each general-use receptacle outlet is rated 180 VA per strap.
- Multi-Outlet Receptacle Assembly
    - In general, a multi-outlet receptacle assembly powers multiple appliances at the same time.
    - For service calculations, you can assume that the rating of 180 VA is applicable for every 5 feet or less.
- Receptacle Service Demand Load
    - The receptacle loads that are not more than 180 VA each can be added to the lighting loads.
    - Loads of fixed multi-outlet receptacle assemblies may also be added.
    - For the said loads, the demand factors in Table 220.11 or 220.13 must be applied in the calculations.

Electric Sign Loads

According to section 600.5(A) of the Code, every commercial occupancy that is accessible to pedestrians must have a 20-ampere branch circuit for the electric sign.

The minimum load for each sign is 1,200 VA. Since the outlet of the sign is a continuous load, the sizing of the feeder load must be 125% of the continuous load.

Practice Questions: Commercial Load Calculations

Instructions: Select the best answer from the given choices.

1. Determine the receptacle load for an office that has a total area of 18,000 ft² and one hundred sixty 15-ampere, 125-volt receptacles.
    a. 18,000 VA
    b. 19,400 VA
    c. 20,000 VA
    d. 21,400 VA
2. What is the required size of a branch-circuit conductor for a 7,000-VA commercial dryer that is rated 240 volts if it is used in a laundry shop?
    a. 6 AWG
    b. 8 AWG
    c. 10 AWG
    d. 12 AWG
3. For the above given commercial dryer, what size should its overcurrent protection device be?
    a. 30 amperes
    b. 60 amperes
    c. 90 amperes
    d. 120 amperes
4. What is the maximum number of receptacles that is permitted for a 15-ampere circuit with a voltage of 120 volts?
    a. 10 receptacles
    b. 15 receptacles
    c. 20 receptacles
    d. 25 receptacles
5. What is the minimum calculated load for the feeder/service conductor of an electrical sign?
    a. 1,000 VA
    b. 1,500 VA
    c. 2,000 VA
    d. 2,500 VA

Answer Key: Commercial Load Calculations
   1. b. 19,400 VA

Based on sections 220.14(K)(1):
$$180\ VA * 160\ receptacles = 28,800\ VA$$

For the load, the first 10,000 VA should be at 100%, while the remaining VA will be at 50%. Therefore:
$$28,000\ VA - 10,000\ VA = 18,800\ VA$$
$$18,800\ VA * 50\% = 9,400\ VA$$

To get the calculated receptacle load for the entire office, just get the sum of the loads:
$$10,000\ VA + 9,400\ VA = 19,400\ VA$$

Another way to obtain the calculated receptacle load is based on section 220.14 (K)(2):
$$18,000\ square\ feet * 1\ VA\ per\ square\ feet = 18,000\ VA$$

Since 19,400 VA is larger than 18,000 VA, the correct answer is choice b.

2. c. 10 AWG
    For this question, use the formula $I = VA \div E$ (where I = current, VA = volt-ampere rating and E = voltage)
$$I = 7,000\ VA \div 240\ volts$$
$$I = 29\ amperes$$

The demand load for the dryer is at 100% because it is used for commercial purposes.

According to Table 310.16, the branch-circuit conductor should be 10-AWG.

3. a. 30 amperes
    Using the same calculation as provided in item no. 2, refer to 240.6(A). Given that the dryer has a 10-AWG branch-circuit conductor, it must have a 30-ampere overcurrent protection device.

4. a. 10 receptacles
   First, determine the total VA load of the circuit:

   $120 \; volts * 15 \; amperes = 1,800 \; VA$

   Next, calculate the maximum count:

   $1,800 \; VA \div 180 \; VA = 10$

   Given this, the maximum number of receptacles of the given circuit is 10.

5. b. 1,500 VA
   According to 220.14(F), an electric sign has a minimum load of 1,200 VA. However, the service conductor for an electric sign should be 125% of its continuous load. Therefore:

   $Minimum \; Calculated \; Load = 1,200 \; VA * 125\%$

   $Minimum \; Calculated \; Load = 1,500 \; VA$

Voltage Drop Calculations

Voltage drop is the product of the current and resistance of a given circuit. Though there is no mandatory requirement in the Code for a specific amount of voltage drop allowed on branch circuits and feeders, the NEC recommendation states that the total voltage drop cannot be more than 5% to ensure the reasonable efficiency level of the operation. Furthermore, the Code suggests that the maximum for branch circuits and feeders should be 3%. This means that if a feeder circuit had 3%, the branch circuit could have 2%—and vice versa. With this, the operating voltage for the loads will still be sufficient despite cable resistance.

For voltage drop calculations, the hardest part is determining the resistance of the circuit. Why? Because the total resistance of the circuit depends on the length, material, and size of the conductors of the circuit.

Before we delve into the formulas that you can use, remember that for voltage drop calculations, every set of parallel conductors in a circuit is considered as only one conductor. The calculations below result in an approximate voltage drop for AC circuits. Factors such as power factor and skin-effect were not considered in the sample calculations below. Lastly, you should not rely on the following formulas when designing large feeders or feeders that are intended for harmonic or inductive loads.

Formulas for a Single-Phase Circuit

For single-phase, this formula based on Ohm's Law may be used to calculate the voltage drop:

$$VD\ 1\emptyset = I * R$$

Where:

$VD\ 1\emptyset$ = voltage drop for a single-phase circuit
I = current of the circuit
R = total resistance of the conductors in the circuit

The current is expressed in amperes, while the value of R can be obtained in Table 8 of NEC Chapter 9 for DC circuits, or Table 9 for AC circuits.

Take a look at the example below for the application of this formula.

> Calculate the voltage drop of two 12-AWG conductors that supply a load of 16 amperes, operates at 120 volts, and is located 100 feet from the panel board.

$VD\ 1\emptyset = I * R$

$VD\ 1\emptyset = 16\ amperes * 0.4\ ohms$

Reminder!

Though the NEC does not require voltage drop for general applications, Article 648 of the Code contains the details about voltage drop requirements for sensitive electronic equipment.

$VD\ 1\emptyset = 6.4\ volts$

Another way of calculating voltage drop is through the formula method. For single-phase circuits, there are two formulas you can use:

- Option 1: $VD\ 1\emptyset = \frac{2 * K * I * L}{CM}$

    Where:

VD 1∅ = voltage drop for a single-phase circuit
K = DC constant
I = current of the circuit
L = length of the circuit in one direction
CM = circular mils of the conductors

In the above-given formula, take note that "K" is a constant that represents the DC resistance for a circular mils conductor which operates at 75°C and has a length of 1,000 feet. For copper conductors, the value of K is 12.9 ohms, while aluminum conductors have a K value of 21.2 ohms. AC circuits may use the K constant if their conductors are not more than 1/0-AWG.

For the circular mil area of the conductor, you can find information about this in Table 8 of the NEC Chapter 9.

- Option 2: $VD\ 1\emptyset = \frac{2*R*I*L}{1,000}$

    Where:

    VD 1∅ = voltage drop for a single-phase circuit
    R = ohms per 1,000 feet of the conductor
    I = current
    L = length of the circuit in one direction

For this formula, "R" can be found in Table 8 of Chapter 9 of the Code. Similar to the first option, the current of the circuit must be expressed in amperes.

Let's go over how you should apply these formulas based on the details provided on the sample question.

Determine the voltage drop on a 240-volt, single-phase circuit that has 8-AWG THWN copper conductors, a current of 28 amperes, and has a distance of 150 feet from the panel board.

$$VD\ 1\emptyset = \frac{2*K*I*L}{CM}$$

$$VD\ 1\emptyset = \frac{2*12.9*28\ amperes*150\ feet}{16{,}510\ circular\ mils}$$

$$VD\ 1\emptyset = 6.5\ volts$$

Formulas for a 3-Phase Circuit

The approach for calculating the voltage drop based on Ohm's Law ($VD = I * R$, wherein VD = voltage drop, I = electric current, R = resistance) cannot be applied to 3-phase circuits. Therefore, you would have to apply the formula method instead.

> **Remember!**
>
> The voltage drop of a single-phase circuit is slightly greater than that of a three-phase circuit because only one of the three conductors of a three-phase circuit is at maximum current at any given time.

- Option 1: $VD\ 3\emptyset = \frac{1.732*K*I*L}{CM}$

    Where:

    VD 3∅ = voltage drop for a three-phase circuit
    K = the constant of Ω per mil foot
    I = electric current
    L = circuit length in one direction
    CM = circular mil

- Option 2:

    Where:

    VD 3∅ = voltage drop for a three-phase circuit
    R = ohms per 1,000 feet of the conductor
    I = electric current
    L = circuit length in one direction

Take a look at the sample voltage drop calculations for a 3-phase circuit using the formulas given above.

> What is the voltage drop on a three-phase branch circuit with a voltage of 208 volts, a current of 33 amperes, a resistance of 0.510 ohms per 1,000 feet, and a distance of 205 feet from the panelboard?
> For this scenario, use the formula: $VD\ 3\emptyset = \frac{1.732 * R * I * L}{1,000}$
> $VD\ 3\emptyset = \frac{1.732 * 0.510\ ohms * 33\ amperes * 205\ feet}{1,000}$
> $VD\ 3\emptyset = 5.98\ volts$

Formulas for Percentage of Voltage Drop

You can also calculate the percentage of voltage drop using equations that are derived from the formula for voltage drop. For example:

Calculate the percentage of voltage drop on a 3-phase feeder circuit that operates at 480 volts, has a current of 135 amperes, two 250-kcmil XHHW aluminum conductors, and is located at a distance of 280 feet from the service equipment to the panel board.

$VD\ 3\emptyset = \frac{1.732 * 21.1\ ohms * 135\ amperes * 280\ feet}{250,000}$

$VD\ 3\emptyset = 5.53\ volts$

$Percent\ of\ VD = \frac{VD\ 3\emptyset}{EL-L} * 100$

$Percent\ of\ VD = \frac{5.53\ volts}{480\ volts} * 100$

$Percent\ of\ VD = 1.15\%$

Practice Questions: Voltage Drop Calculations

Instructions: Select the best answer from the given choices.

1. What is the voltage drop on a 240-volt single-phase circuit that is 160 feet from the panel board, and uses 6-AWG copper conductors to supply 44 amperes to the load?
    a. 6.9 volts
    b. 7.5 volts
    c. 11.3 volts

d. 13.8 volts
2. A 208-volt 3-phase circuit with a load of 100 amperes is located 80 feet from the panel board. It has 1-AWG conductors made of aluminum. What is the voltage drop for this circuit?
   a. 2.1 volts
   b. 3.5 volts
   c. 4.9 volts
   d. 5.3 volts
3. Determine the voltage drop of two 12-AWG conductors that are used to supply a 16-ampere, 120-volt load that uses 200 feet of wire to connect to a power supply that is 100 feet away.
   a. 2.2 volts
   b. 6.4 volts
   c. 10.6 volts
   d. 14.8 volts
4. If the voltage drop is not more than 3%, what is the maximum length of a 4-AWG THHN conductor that serves as the connection between the panel board and a 35-KVA, 480-volt, 3-phase transformer?
   a. 80 feet
   b. 160 feet
   c. 320 feet
   d. 640 feet
5. Without exceeding the recommended voltage drop of the NEC, what should be the 3-phase load if it will be connected to the power supply using 220 feet of 8-AWG THHN conductors, rated 480 volts?
   a. 20 KVA
   b. 30 KVA
   c. 40 KVA
   d. 50 KVA

Answer Key: Voltage Drop Calculations
1. a. 6.9 volts

   For this question, use the formula $VD\ 1\emptyset = \frac{2*K*I*L}{CM}$

   Don't forget to refer to NEC Table 8 for the circular mil area of the conductors.

   $VD\ 1\emptyset = \frac{2 * 12.9\ \Omega * 44\ A * 160\ ft.}{26,240\ CM}$

   $VD\ 1\emptyset = 6.9\ volts$

2. b. 3.5 volts
   After checking Table 8 for the circular mil area for the 1-AWG conductors, apply this formula: $VD\ 3\emptyset = \frac{1.732 * K * I * L}{CM}$

   $VD\ 3\emptyset = \frac{1.732 * 21.2\ \Omega * 100\ A * 80\ ft.}{83,690\ CM}$

   $VD\ 3\emptyset = 3.5\ volts$

3. b. 6.4 volts
   Use the formula $VD = I * R$. You can find the value of resistance using Table 9 of NEC Chapter 9, where you can derive a resistance value of 0.4 ohms for the 200 feet of wire.

$VD = 16\ amperes * 0.4\ ohms$

$VD = 6.4\ volts$

4. d. 640 feet
   Start by deriving the formula for the length of the wire from the formula for voltage drop in a 3-phase circuit.
   $Length = \frac{VD * CM}{1.732 * I * K}$

   Since the voltage drop percentage is 3%, the value of VD for the equation is:

$VD = 480\ volts * 3\%$

$VD = 14.4\ volts$

   Next, refer to Table 8 of NEC Chapter 9 for the value of CM. The table indicates that the 4-AWG THHN conductor is 41,740 circular mils. Since this is a copper conductor, the value of K should be 12.9.

   For the current flow, divide the load of the transformer by 1.732 and the voltage rating.
   $I = \frac{35,000\ VA}{1.732 * 480\ volts}$

$I = 42\ amperes$

   Combining all these elements:

$$Length = \frac{14.4\ volts * 41{,}740\ circular\ mils}{1.732 * 42\ amperes * 12.9}$$

$$Length = 640\ feet$$

5. **c. 40,000 volt-amps**

   First, use the formula for the voltage drop of 3-phase circuits to determine its current flow.

   $$I = \frac{VD * CM}{1.732 * K * L}$$

   Based on the Code, the maximum recommended percentage of voltage drop for branch-circuit conductors is 3%. Therefore, the value of VD is:

   $$VD = 480\ volts * 3\%$$

   $$VD = 14.4\ volts$$

   For the value of CM, check Table 8 of NEC Chapter 9. According to the table, an 8-AWG THHN copper wire is 16,510 circular mils. For the value of K, use the constant 12.9 for copper.

   Next, solve for the current flow of the 3-phase circuit.

   $$I = \frac{14.4\ volts * 16{,}510\ circular\ mils}{1.732 * 12.9 * 220\ feet}$$

   $$I = 48.36\ amperes$$

   To find out the load of the 3-phase circuit, apply this formula:

   $$Power = 1.732 * current * voltage$$

   $$Power = 1.732 * 48.36\ amperes * 480\ volts$$

   $$Power = 40.2\ KVA$$

   You can drop the decimal numbers for this, so the correct answer is 40 KVA.

www.ingramcontent.com/pod-product-compliance
Lightning Source LLC
Chambersburg PA
CBHW081448070526
44586CB00019B/2265